Terry
Waite

WOMEN OF FAITH SERIES

✓ *Amy Carmichael*
✓ *Corrie ten Boom*
   Florence Nightingale
   Gladys Aylward
   Isobel Kuhn
   Mary Slessor

MEN OF FAITH SERIES

   Borden of Yale
   Brother Andrew
   C. S. Lewis
   Charles Finney
   Charles Spurgeon
   Eric Liddell
✓ *George Muller*
   Hudson Taylor
   Jim Elliot
   Jonathan Goforth
✓ *John Hyde*
   John Wesley
   Samuel Morris
✓ *Terry Waite*
   William Carey

   John and Betty Stam

Terry Waite

Trevor Barnes

BETHANY HOUSE PUBLISHERS
MINNEAPOLIS, MINNESOTA 55438
A Ministry of Bethany Fellowship, Inc.

Terry Waite
Trevor Barnes

Library of Congress Catalog Card Number 92-81655

ISBN 1–55661–302–2

Originally published in English by Marshall Pickering, an
imprint of HarperCollins Publishers, Ltd. under the title

Terry Waite

Published by Bethany House Publishers
A Ministry of Bethany Fellowship, Inc.
6820 Auto Club Road, Minneapolis, Minnesota 55438

Printed in the United States of America

Contents

1. Homecoming 7
2. Scenes From a Provincial Life 17
3. First Stirrings of Vocation 37
4. Home and Abroad 59
5. Active Service 77
6. A New Departure 93
7. Into the Fire 115
8. Dangerous Liaisons 135
9. No Regrets, No Sentimentality,
   No Self-pity 149

1

Homecoming

The church envoy looked distinctly crumpled as he stepped out into the cold rain of RAF Lyneham on November 19, 1991. Had he any choice in the matter he might have taken something more impressive to wear on his return to Britain and to freedom after nearly five years of captivity in Lebanon. But choice had been in short supply during the 1,763 days and nights of his detention, so he contented himself with wearing what he had been given—a battered old anorak, a hastily borrowed sweater, and a shirt so absurdly tight that it refused to button at the neck, leaving his tie (a very English touch) loosely adrift.

Did it matter? Not a bit. Once the world had reaccustomed itself to the familiar bearded figure waving to the crowd, all it saw was the smile. A smile that cut through the autumn chill, and but for the hint of pain in the flashing eyes, caused the strain of those years of separation to vanish in an instant. Terry Waite was back home.

Canon Sam Van Cullin, one of the last people to see Waite before he set out on his perilous journey, was now one of the first to express the general sense of relief: "All of us in the Anglican Communion have been aware of the plight of Terry Waite," he said. "Millions of prayers, literally, have been offered for his safety each and every day since he was taken captive in the course of his work."

In Cheshire, the county of his birth, the cathedral bells exploded with thanksgiving in jubilation at the return of a famous son. The Bishop of Chester asked for special services, and added, "The news is wonderful. I am filled with emotion—overwhelmingly thankful to God, thrilled with excitement, and delighted for Terry's mother, wife, and family."

Jubilation was the mood of the moment. Photographs of Terry Waite's meeting with his former employer, Robert Runcie, show the two men roaring with laughter and sheer delight at the safe return. Characteristically Terry managed a joke. "Lord Runcie, I presume," he said, defying some gloomy predictions that his arrival on British soil would be as a broken man.

The vast inner reserves of strength of which friends had spoken so often appeared intact. Waite's faith in God had carried him through deprivation, torture, and loneliness, and, so it seemed to many onlookers that afternoon on the airfield, had deposited him on home ground all the stronger for it.

Then he took to the podium to deliver a speech (without notes) to the waiting journalists assembled in the drafty RAF hangar. In true Waite fashion he had others in mind. "Ladies and gentlemen," he began, "I think you can imagine that after 1,763 days in chains it's an overwhelming experience to come back and receive your greetings. From the bottom of my heart, thank you for turning out on such an awful day—but a typically English day—and thank you so much for your welcome."

The thanks were directed to those in and out of the public eye. To the Secretary-General of the United Nations for his hard and persistent work to seek a resolution to the problem of all hostages who had been detained in the Middle East. To the current and the past Archbishops of Canterbury for their care and concern. To the Foreign Secretary for quiet diplomacy as he "walked on eggshells in a territory that is difficult and dangerous." To the small and industrious staff of Lambeth Palace with whom he had once been so familiar.

And then a moment of humor (and an explanation for his unusual appearance) as he addressed the men who had flown him home. "Of course, what could a homecoming be without the RAF?" he wondered aloud. "I can tell you one thing, that when I left Hezbollah [the radical Islamic group responsible for his kidnapping and detention] yesterday afternoon, they did their best to fit me out with a sweater and a pair of trousers, but they couldn't find a pair of shoes my size. So when I got to Cyprus late at night all I could say to the RAF was, 'Can you find a pair of size 14's?' and within half an hour they contacted the Navy and provided me with two barges! Thanks to the RAF."

Within the space of a few moments here was Terry Waite playing to the gallery as of old. And by any standards it was an impressive performance. The fervor, the humor, and the compassion—in a homecoming that had confounded even the most optimistic expectations.

But as the speech progressed beyond the formalities, the true character of the man emerged. Although he was the last British hostage to return, he had left behind him in Beirut three Americans (one with whom he had shared a cell, Terry Anderson). It was with these men that his thoughts now lay. Thanks to a special plea they had made to the guards, they had succeeded in having Anderson's chains released so that at least he was able to walk around the room in which he had been confined. The Americans, too, he was able to assure his audience, would shortly be freed. For their (and his) captors he had a message that was firm but understated.

"On this day," he continued, "it would not be right for me to leave this podium without remembering all those in the Middle East who are held captive. It is wrong to hold people in such a way. It is self-defeating, and those who do it fall well below civilized standards of behavior, no matter who they are, no matter what nationality or what organization they belong to.

"We have lived in these last years through the appalling sufferings of the people of Lebanon. We have been in the midst of shelling. We have seen people die and be killed in the most brutal ways. We know that the people of Lebanon have suffered greatly, and those from whom I have just come can be assured that we in the Church will not rest until all are freed and there is justice and peace brought to people who deserve a better deal."

With that mildest of rebukes he embodied all the authority of his Christian calling. Here was a man who could understand the desperation of his kidnappers but not condone their action; a man who could forgive them their harsh treatment of him but counsel them not to commit such wickedness again: "It is wrong to hold people in such a way . . . those who do it fall well below civilized standards of behavior." The restraint of those remarks! How much it spoke of the man!

As a commentator at the time remarked, Waite's behavior during those first few hours of freedom illustrated what Ernest Hemingway described as the characteristic of the true hero—"grace under pressure."

What was truly remarkable was that he showed no trace of hatred or bitterness. Other, lesser men could have been corroded by the experience. But Terry Waite showed to the world that his Christian faith had been tested to the limit and not found wanting. It was Christian love in action. Not sentimentality but hard-edged, sacrificial love. The ability to rise above anger and to transform the horror of the past four and a half years into something good.

Now Terry Waite was back in his element once again—as a humanitarian and Christian soldier doing his bit to fight injustice and cruelty in the world. Although he had paid a heavy price for it.

Just how deprived he had been in those terrible years was illustrated by a remarkable story. Terry Waite held the audience spellbound as he told it: "I was kept in total and complete isolation for four years," he said, describing an imprisonment all the more terrifying for being indefinite. "I saw no one and spoke to no one apart from a cursory word with my guards when they brought me food. And then one day, out of the blue, a guard came with a postcard. The card showed a stained-glass window from Bedford showing John Bunyan in jail."

As he spoke, one woman watched him on her television screen with particular interest. And eventually Mrs. Joy Brodier of Bedford could contain herself no longer. "That's my card. That's my card!" she shouted. A fifteen-cent postcard bought by her and her husband, Graham, to mark Terry Waite's birthday, and addressed simply: Terry Waite, c/o Hezbollah, Party of God, Beirut, Lebanon, had against all odds arrived at its destination and illuminated Terry's darkest hour.

It was not hard to imagine how the arrival of a postcard from England might have raised his spirits. But as he spoke he had no idea of the identity of Mr. and Mrs. Brodier. They were total strangers to him, anonymous fellow Christians who had merely wished to express their continuing concern in this novel and striking way. And he had indeed been moved by it.

"I looked at that card," he said, "and I thought, 'My word, Bunyan, you're a lucky fellow. You've got a window out of which you can look. You can see the sky, and here am I in a dark room. You've got pen and ink; you can write, but here am I, I've got nothing, and you've got your own clothes and a table and chair.' And I turned the card over and there was a message from someone I didn't know simply saying: 'We remember. We shall not forget. We shall continue to pray for you and to work for all people who are detained around the world.' "

Mrs. Brodier made light of the incident the next day when the national newspapers tracked her down for the details of this charming human interest story. "I thought it must be worth a try just for the sake of a fifteen-cent stamp," she said. But the action was more significant than that, and its significance was not lost on the church envoy himself.

"I thought the picture would speak to him as much as the message," said Mrs. Brodier. "John Bunyan was in prison in Bedford for his faith, and through his imprisonment came his great work, *The Pilgrim's Progress*. Pilgrim went through the Slough of Despond and was imprisoned in Doubting Castle, and would have felt all the emotions Terry would be going through, so I thought the picture would slip in another message as well."

Indeed it had. And as a result, that phrase: "My word, Bunyan, you're a lucky fellow," was surely destined to be quoted for years to come.

What the action showed also was the genuine love and respect Terry Waite could inspire among men and women he had never even met. It showed the power of Christian hope, which had been his constant (though sorely tried) companion through the blackest of times. "Never despise those simple actions," he said. "Something, somewhere will get through to the people you are concerned about, as it got through to me and my fellows eventually."

He could have been talking about prayer itself.

So with that stirring speech Terry Waite took his leave of the public, and with waving arms and beaming smile made his way to his wife and family, to a longed-for reunion out of the glare of the cameras.

———

There was, however, to be a dramatic postscript to the brief outline of Waite's personal agony. Many months later he was to reveal to Barbara Walters of

ABC News a fact that he had hitherto kept secret. And even the super-professional Miss Walters could not disguise a moment of astonishment as she scooped the world with this unexpected disclosure.

To an incredulous audience, Terry Waite let it be known that at a critical moment in his captivity he had an opportunity to escape but that he had deliberately let it pass.

The moment had come during a routine visit to the bathroom. His chains had been unlocked, his arms and legs released, and he was ushered into the room still blindfolded. He closed the door, removed the blindfold, and saw on the top of the toilet back a loaded gun. He now had a terrible choice. Armed with this weapon he could surely escape. With a short burst of lethal gunfire he could bring the years of pain and separation to an end. But to do that he would have to be prepared to kill.

There was a moment's hesitation as he reviewed the principles that had guided his life to this point. "I'd argued with the kidnappers long before I was kidnapped myself," he told Miss Walters, "and I used to say to them, 'It's absolutely futile for you to keep engaging in violent activities. It's self-defeating. Give it up. Use your brains. Renounce violence.' "

The dangerous illogicality of an armed escape now hit him with the force of a lifetime's conviction. How could he contemplate the very violence he had condemned in others for so long? The answer, of course, was that he could not. It would have been a denial of the gospel message. A denial of the saving power of God's love.

"I must stand by what I believe," he said to himself as he put his blindfold back on, and summoned his guards to take him back to a lonely cell and imprisonment without limit.

If confirmation of his Christian self-sacrifice were needed, here it was. No, he was no saint, he told his interviewer. A hero, then? To be sure, Terry Waite would never suggest such a thing.

Others just might.

2

Scenes From a Provincial Life

Terry Waite's role as "Archbishop of Canterbury's Special Envoy" is a misleading one. It is a product of the media, not a title of the Church's making. True, it served him well during his much publicized trips abroad to help seek the release of those detained unjustly, but nowhere is it listed as his official job description. And yet in one sense the title is appropriate.

Through this hugely attractive envoy, whose face has become immediately recognizable to everyone, those who have lost contact with the Church are suddenly reminded of its presence in the world; those who long ago lost interest in it sit up for once and take notice; and those who have lost hope in it are encouraged. Simplicity, integrity, and humanity are Terry Waite's hallmarks—goodness allied with strength in a powerful combination—and to embody those qualities so publicly is surely the most a church, any church, can expect its envoy to do.

Not that he is without his critics, who accuse him of being foolish and naive in thinking he can achieve results by force of principle as opposed to force of arms (or money). Those same critics point to his last mission to Lebanon as proof that he had judged the situation badly, misread the signs, and was acting as a simple child in a grown-up's world. And, they add, how many hostages did Terry Waite actually release compared to the vast numbers in jails throughout the world? How much of an impact did he really make on the world's suffering and injustice? They are questions easy to ask but hard to answer. We can, however, only guess how those he did release would reply. And at least he tried—at no small risk to himself.

He often said that every time he embarked on a mission he did so in the full knowledge that he himself could be taken prisoner at any time—a prediction which proved horribly accurate in Beirut. So why did he do it? What made him take the risks?

The following pages suggest an answer. Terry Waite himself, after a lengthy convalescence, will fill in the fine detail, but in the interim and in the words of family, friends, and colleagues, what emerges even here is a lifetime spent in the service of his Christian faith following a vocation which, with God's help, he has made uniquely his own.

Terence Hardy Waite was born on May 31, 1939, in the village of Bollington near Macclesfield in Cheshire, the son of Lena and Thomas, a police constable. When he was nine months old the family moved to Henbury at the other side of Macclesfield, and stayed there until he was seven, when they moved again to Styal near Wilmslow. In bald outline it does not read like the account of an exciting boyhood, and Terry Waite himself always longed to escape the bounds of what he feared might become a narrow and restricting provincial life.

As a boy he chose bicycle trips as a means of escape: long solitary journeys along the highways and byways of his native Cheshire and beyond. On one occasion he returned home with a surprise in store for his mother. "I've just flown over our house," he said, to Lena's evident shock. Dismissing it first as a joke she eventually believed him when he regaled her with the whole story. Apparently he had taken himself and his bicycle (bought with the proceeds of a paper route) off to Manchester Airport. There, with the easy charm and friendliness that was to mark his later years, he fell into conversation with a man who owned a plane. The invitation to come for a spin was not refused, and so it was that the young Terry Waite came to be flying over his parents' house. Not quite so exciting as the international trips he would later be embarking on, but not bad for a teenager!

Already the incident goes some way toward explaining his personality—a strange mixture of the solitary and the gregarious. At home with people from all different walks of life, relaxed and engaging in their company but equally at home alone. He spent a lot of time reading and listening to the radio, and planning those bicycle trips that would take him away for hours on end.

One such trip took him farther afield and led to his first appearance on television—perhaps the earliest indication of the celebrity he was later to achieve. It took place around 1955, although his mother, who remembers the incident clearly enough, is rather hesitant about the date.

"That's Terry," she cried, as she watched the TV in disbelief. And she called to his sister, Diana, to come and see. By the time Diana had made it to the sitting room the young Terry had vanished from the screen, but it had been him all right. "There he was," his mother remembers, "standing on the platform at Vienna railway station checking his watch against the station clock. You couldn't miss him. He was head and shoulders above the rest of the crowd."

So what was Terry Waite doing there? Had hostages been taken in the Tyrol? Had the young troubleshooter been summoned to sort out a spot of bother in central Europe? Not at all. He had merely been on a European cycling holiday, and an early children's program had happened to film him halfway through it. He had taken the train and boat to the continent, and set off alone to cycle around the Black Forest. Standing there on the station in Austria he had merely been caught up in the filming.

The story confirms his lifelong love of travel, and a restlessness of character that had become apparent much earlier in smaller ways. He has never forgotten the disappointment he felt when his family was unable to afford the fifteen pounds needed to send him on a school trip to France with his classmates. His brother David, seven years Terry's junior, recalls it too: "Our Dad was the village bobby and Mum didn't work, so with only one wage coming in they had to tell Terry that they couldn't afford to send him away. Terry was very upset by that and felt that his big chance to travel had come and gone. It seems ironic, now that he must have gone around the world several times. But I think it was the very thing that stoked up the fires and made him all the more determined to travel later on."

But if the airplane incident and the Austrian trip give early indications of the Waite career, another incident highlights an aspect of his life that has played every bit as important a role in his formation. It illustrates his lifelong attachment to the Church.

His mother takes up the story: "He always wanted to go to church. For as long as I can remember—even when he was a tiny boy. The local church was just up the road about five minutes, but Diana was a baby and my husband was on duty in the police force, and I couldn't always take Terry along. But he still wanted to go, even though he wasn't quite four at the time. He had gotten friendly with an old gentleman who lived locally. He was a regular churchgoer and he told us he would be only too glad to take Terry along with him on Sunday mornings. At the time we had a long driveway leading from the house to a set of double gates where Terry would wait impatiently for the man to turn up. He was always under strict instructions to wait on this side of the gate until the gentleman appeared.

"But one Sunday the man was late. The church bells were ringing and ringing. Terry was waiting and waiting, and there was no sign of the man at all. I knew nothing of all this of course, and as the man had not telephoned to let us know, I assumed he had arrived as arranged. The service was about to begin and Terry looked down the road for the man. No sign of him. At that point Terry just got it into his head to set off. On his own. All by himself at the age of three, and the youngest one there, I'll bet! He loved the church, and I also remember him being the youngest to get a Sunday school prize."

By the time the family had moved to Styal, Terry was already an enthusiastic member of the church choir, and was always to remember the encouragement and advice his father had given him: "Once you start a job, stick at it until you've finished." It would be easy, and not necessarily a mistake, to see in that advice one of the guiding principles of the church envoy's later life. Commitment to the job at hand and the honoring of promises made could well have been the Waite family motto.

Terry was also receiving instruction for confirmation at about this time, and the circumstances surrounding it are worth noting since they reveal an important duality in his nature.

The confirmation classes were held in a room above a pub. And far from being an inappropriate place to conduct such serious matters, it was according to Terry Waite the ideal spot. Learning about the Lord and His ways in isolation from the world outside was not for him. His Christianity has always been active and involved with the lives of ordinary people. So what better place to be instructed in the faith than in an upper room where the sounds of laughter and friendship could spill over. Terry's younger brother recalls the influence the Church had on his life. At the time not particularly "religious" himself, he was always being encouraged by his big brother to come along to the "Tin Tabernacle" where Terry was by now a regular worshiper. "As a matter of fact," says David, "I've got Terry to thank for my name!

"I was born prematurely, and Terry arrived back from church one Sunday to find he had a brother—a very sick brother, as things turned out, and one who wasn't expected to live for very long. Mum and Dad felt they had to get me christened as soon as possible, so they sent for the vicar. The only problem was that they had no time to think of a name. Terry barged in fresh from Sunday school where he'd been studying the story of David and Jonathan. He put forward his suggestion, my parents agreed, and so here I am as David John Waite. But I must say I'm ever so grateful that he hadn't been listening to the story of David and Goliath!"

Religion was not a major component of the home, according to David, so it is something of a mystery to him where Terry got his yearning for it. "I don't think for one minute my father would have said he was a Christian in the way I understand it now," he says. "My mother had a strong faith, but I think it was a case of when one partner in a marriage doesn't appear to have that faith, the other partner drops away in order to keep the peace. Or just because it isn't possible to worship together. I think that's what happened in our family."

Being brought up in a settled community played an important part in the lives of both brothers. It provided the stable base to which the boys could return from their adventures. That, along with Terry's developing Christian faith, gave him a core of certainty and solidity that would support him through everything he was later to do.

To David, Terry was always an excellent and exciting companion. Seven years older, he was now at an age when he could leave his brother behind if he chose to, but often he took him along, impressing him to no end. Even on simple trips to Manchester by train Terry would talk about his bicycle rides, point out things of interest, and give all the details of his latest escapades. "He just had the knack for making life terribly exciting," says David. "When you were with him you got this terrific charge from him, and things became stimulating and full of incident."

Despite his capacity for seriousness and solitude, the young Terry Waite was not above a little mischief—a potentially hazardous enterprise for the eldest son of the village policeman. "I remember one occasion in winter," his brother says. "It had been alleged that a snowball had been posted through someone's letter box. It certainly was never conclusively proven that Terry was the culprit, but he was certainly with the group that had a hand in the affair. When I say he used to go about in a gang, today's connotation throws up the wrong image, but there were certainly a few of them who used to go about together and who weren't above the odd prank or two.

"The thing was that they'd all scuttle away to hide, but when somebody looked out of the window all that could be seen was the outline of one boy standing shoulder high above the rest. And so people would immediately come rushing around to our house and complain to my parents that they'd seen such and such a thing happening, and though they couldn't be sure who all the guilty parties were, they could be quite confident that Terry was among them. A very embarrassing moment for my father, the official upholder of law and order."

Thomas Waite himself was, according to David, a great disciplinarian. He believed that as a police family they should uphold the very highest standards. He was not a father to lay down the law in a heavy-handed sort of way, but he had definite rules, which the children thought it wise to obey. The atmosphere of authority in the home was difficult to avoid because the house was physically attached to the police station. Very often strangers would be seen wandering through the house, and the family lived a semi-public life.

The responsibilities of their father's position were frequently felt in their everyday lives. Many were the times that the family prepared for an outing, only to be told by Dad that police business meant calling it off. "I can still remember the sheer disappointment of it all—even to this day," says David. "There was the time when we were all set for a day out and Dad was called away at the last minute. The trip was canceled, and he actually brought a man back to the house. He took him out to the garden, sat him down in one of our deck chairs and gave him a drink. It turned out that the man had attempted to commit suicide in Styal woods, but somebody had reported the incident in time and Dad was able to take charge."

In such a household where the confidences of strangers were regularly on display, trust and discretion were instilled from an early age. The boys were schooled to keep to themselves everything they had witnessed at home. No confidences were broken, no secrets divulged. And David would not be alone in thinking that such early training was of inestimable value in the work Terry chose to do. "I'm absolutely positive that any confidence given to him will not be breached."

The family was well-liked in the area, and on a trip back to Styal—the first for over a decade—David discovered their old house still standing but empty, and referred to by all those old enough to remember as "The Waite House."

Thomas Waite remained a constable all his life, and according to his younger son refused to climb up the ladder by constantly getting more convictions. He took the view that it was better to try to caution people, to warn them away from doing the wrong thing, without having to drag matters through the courts. "Of course it didn't earn him any stars," says David, "but it did win him a lot of respect." He believes that both boys inherited their father's sense of fair-mindedness and gentle (but firm) concern. The warmhearted father and the disciplinarian went hand in hand, and both boys learned to appreciate the blend of paternal qualities. "Nobody is more secure," says David, "than when they have boundaries in which they know they can work. Terry and I knew that we were safe within those boundaries, but that if we went beyond them we were liable to come under the wrath of our father."

At Stockton Heath Secondary Modern School Terry was an excellent Head Boy, although he later confessed that he grew rather weary of his studies and longed to be out and about pursuing a career that would involve action and travel. He was a popular lad, with the usual range of sporting interests and hobbies, and with a strong patriotic streak in him even then, had half an eye on a life in the Army.

Although it was in many ways an ordinary and uneventful school career, Terry Waite's inner life was developing to a remarkable degree. In particular he was nursing a personality that united two opposing forces. One was his great capacity for action and fun (for some bizarre reason best known to himself, stilt-walking was one of the pursuits the young Terry was seen to take up), and the other was his great capacity for stillness and self-reliance. And alongside both, most importantly of all, was his Christian faith, which was steadily maturing to a degree that was to make a profound impression on older and more experienced clergy and laypeople all over the world.

Christianity was something Terry was beginning to take with the utmost seriousness while all the time wearing it lightly. He carried it with him in the most natural of ways, trying to make it influence his life at every turn. An incident related by his younger brother illustrates Terry's remarkable maturity as much as it demonstrates his complete lack of self-consciousness.

"We both shared a room at home," David recalls, "and one night he came in to tell me that he had just been to a meeting, and that he'd experienced something that had touched him deeply. Now whether that was the moment of his own personal encounter with Christ I don't know, but it was clearly something that had moved him greatly and that he wanted to share. He came over to me—a young lad of seven or eight—and told me that God had touched his life in a very special way, and that if I ever felt like making that step he would be there to encourage me. And he would be on hand to help me through it and tell me what I should do. Every night he used to pray silently by his bedside (I know he was very fond of the Prayer Book) and he had no qualms about praying while I was in the room—a typically horrible younger brother asking why he was bothering to pray when there was no one there! But I grew out of that stage and Terry's example became very important to me."

Anyone who has seen Terry Waite discussing his faith in front of the microphones or the television cameras of the world's media might easily suspect that this is part of some carefully controlled public relations strategy. That it is all "put on" for the sake of the radio or the television. Surely David's story proves the reverse. Isn't the depth of his attachment to the Lord clearly shown by the touching picture of the young adolescent kneeling in silent devotion, patiently resisting the childish taunts of a younger brother, and basing all he did on the bedrock of the Gospel message?

But a footnote for those who fear for David's own salvation! Some of the influence of the older brother eventually did rub off, but led him in quite a different direction. Where David was attracted by the "low" church, Pentecostal branch, Terry is more at home in the "high" Anglo-Catholic traditions. The formal structures of the Orthodox Church he finds particularly appealing. The traditions that stretch back over the centuries, the icons representing the great figures in the life of the Church, the candles representing the ever-present light of God in what seem the most hopeless of times, exert a strong and enduring fascination.

Indeed Terry has often expressed his irritation at some of the developments of the modern style of worship. He once said he regretted the fact that to enter some Anglican churches nowadays is to step into something strange and unfamiliar, where the orders of service have changed so much that you no longer feel at home. The Orthodox liturgy, on the other hand, gives him a known fixed point, a link with generations of believers and a discipline within which he can be free. And in this there are echoes of David's earlier observation that security is to be found within distinct boundaries—the lesson their father taught them both.

"Another thing our father taught us," says David, "was never to look down on anyone and never to be overawed by anyone either. We were taught to respect everyone we met—whether the grandest man in the village or a tramp in the street." That advice too seems to have filtered down to Terry. When he was released from captivity he was as much at home with the ordinary people who turned out to greet him in Cyprus or in his adopted village of Blackheath in South London as he was with the Foreign Secretary and the two Archbishops who met him at the Lyneham air base. Whether he is working with world figures on an international stage or helping to distribute food to the homeless during the seasonal Crisis at Christmas campaigns, he retains his same basic approach of care and concern for all. "Our dad was a man of great wisdom really," says David, "and Terry picked up a lot from him. Honesty, dependability, trustworthiness, discretion. Dad never talked to us much about his work, just as Terry didn't reveal much of what went on during his missions."

Undoubtedly, though, that love of secrecy—more than a touch of the cloak and dagger—was part of his undoing in his last mission to Beirut, where he was hopelessly compromised by American secret agents. Discretion is one thing, relishing secrets for their own sake and for the excitement they can bring is quite another. The danger for him was that behind the secrets he did know were other secrets he did not, dangerous secrets of which he would not for one moment have approved. While he was using all his Christian effort to seek the release of British and American hostages, Colonel Oliver North, a trusted aide within the American administration, was making secret deals of his own.

In what was later to be known as "Irangate," arms were to be secretly shipped to Iran in exchange for the release of hostages in the Middle East and for cash that would be used to fund resistance to the communist regime in Nicaragua. Terry Waite himself said frequently that it was wrong to trade arms or money for lives, and at no point in this discreditable episode did he actively connive in the process. But as time went on he began to realize that his good faith and his good offices were being manipulated by others intent on bargains of a different kind.

Should he have realized much earlier? Was the sheer excitement of playing so high-profile a role in the full glare of the world's media blinding him to the reality of life? The charge of naivety, even of gullibility, begins to look more credible in the light of known events. But then hindsight is a very precise science.

And is anyone perfect in every way? Certainly not Terry Waite, who would be the first to agree. He is a larger-than-life character, and larger-than-life characters have larger-than-life faults alongside their larger-than-life virtues. In men and women who have made their mark in the world there are often uncomfortable traits that make them what they are, and we must accept them whole or not at all.

Impatience and temper are two personality "defects" that Terry's younger brother has noted. "He's tolerant up to a point," says David, "and then the fuse blows. He'll go red in the face, and storm out of the room waving his arms around. It will be a big explosion while it lasts, but it's soon over. What he's learned to do over the years is to keep his emotions in check, which is all part of his professionalism."

And it would be wrong to think that impatience and a temper can wipe out other aspects of personality. They are merely two facets that go into making the extraordinarily complex individual Terry Waite is. Focusing on them alone, however, overlooks his great good humor and sense of fun, which are liable to spill over when the seriousness of the moment has passed.

But to return to the early formation of Terry Waite, whom we have left so far as a young schoolboy fond of cycling and rather impatient with schoolwork. For David he was always a few steps ahead, a slightly unreachable sort of figure who was clearly out of the ordinary in an indefinable sort of way, but not, as far as David could see, marked down for the sort of fame he was subsequently to achieve.

His first attempt to break free of the provinciality of his early life led to upset in the family, and to what David remembers as "the great debate." Terry was clearly bored with academic studies (although in later life he was to resume his studies, and to regret not having devoted himself to them much earlier and with greater effort), and his impatience for adventure led him to consider a career in the Navy. The family was not at all enthusiastic, and for some time an uneasy air of tension hung around in the Waite household. Terry, however, was determined to go, and ticket in hand he made his way to Styal station accompanied by a sad but forbearing mother. "The train pulled in," she remembers. "He put his hand on the carriage door and I said to him, 'Well, are you going or not?' and he paused a moment, looked at me and said, 'No, I'm not,' and he came back with me."

Lena Waite laughs at the story now, but there was clearly much relief that her sixteen-year-old son resisted the call of the sea. Eventually the call to travel could be resisted no longer, and the family knew it. So a year later, after discussions in the home, Terry convinced his parents that a life in the Army was what he really wanted. They agreed. This time when the train taking him to the barracks in Caterham pulled into the station, there was no turning back.

But this new beginning proved to be nothing more than a false start. After a short time in the Guards, Terry was taken ill with a mysterious condition. A strange rash had appeared on his body, and military doctors were initially at a loss to diagnose the problem. He was sent to a military hospital for a long period until, bafflement still prevailing, he was finally discharged and sent home. Within weeks the rash disappeared and he was duly returned to the barracks. The condition had vanished and the doctor declared him fit to return.

No more than a couple of weeks passed before the strange complaint erupted once again. This time, after a period of consultation and enquiry, the doctors stumbled on to the cause. Terry was allergic to the dye in the uniform. Khaki (a dark mustard, heavy-duty, very itchy sort of cloth that was standard issue in those days) caused Terry to break out in an irritating blemish that, although comparatively minor, put an effective end to a career in the Forces.

The five-month period in the military hospital was a formative one for Terry Waite. It was an opportunity for quiet and reflection. No more long solitary bicycle trips now. Just time to take stock. To look into himself and to put to himself the questions that really mattered.

For many young men of his age it could have been an opportunity missed, a tiresome interruption to a life of "getting out and about." But with Terry it was a key transforming moment. Remember, here was a young man who could not bear to be in one spot for more than a moment, a fellow who given the slightest chance would be off embarking on some new scheme far away from home. Now here he was confined to one spot for a period that for all he knew had no end. It was apparently an indefinite period of incarceration.

His brother David has had ample time to reflect on the similarities between that time in the military hospital in England and the period of trial in an underground cell in the wasteland of Beirut. Two months after Terry's disappearance he had this to say:

"We pray with the children every night for Terry's safe return. We pray that he will come out of it all unscathed. But if we go back to that time in the hospital I think we can see parallels with the current situation. I honestly think that what he is going through now [in 1987] will be a similar period of reflection for him. I think he will come out of it a different man than when he went in. I think some of the rough corners will have rubbed off him a bit and some of that restless energy may be tamed. Maybe he'll calm down a bit more. That energy's been put to good use, but maybe he just needs to slow it down a bit and take life a little more gently. I don't think either of us is particularly emotional. We both have deep feelings but we tend not to show them. And I suppose in general we're not a very demonstrative family. But there is a bond between us. I suppose it's the typical stiff-upper-lip British thing not to say what you feel about someone until he's in a tight situation, but I'm very fond of him. And I think he is of me. And I do feel that this period will be crucial in his life as it will be in ours."

The concern in David's voice was easy to hear. And yet he was clearly hopeful that all would be well. He was certain that God was in full control and that He would not desert Terry in his time of trial. And, as during the time of enforced recuperation at the military hospital in the South of England, he felt that Terry himself would inevitably be drawing strength from the presence of the Lord.

Meanwhile, in the army ward the young recruit lay immobile and listless. Army chaplains and representatives of the Church Army (the social and evangelistic wing of the Church of England) came and went and worked their way into Terry's thinking. After a time a new plan began to hatch. He would join the Church. Not as a priest but as a member of this persuasive band of lay enthusiasts, committed to serving the Lord but not restricted to remaining tied to one parish. The new career move initially startled the family but met eventually with their full approval.

Terry decided to leave the Guards and to train for the Church Army. He swapped one uniform for another—not unlike that of the Salvation Army—and became affiliated with an organization whose aim, despite its name, is Christian action in the pursuit of peace.

The uniform did not contain khaki dye, it's true. But there was far more to his decision than that. And the decision itself was to set the seal on the future course of the whole of his professional and spiritual life to come.

3

First Stirrings of Vocation

T here was no denying that the military ring of the Church Army was some compensation for the promise of adventure that the Guards had held out to Terry but which had now been abruptly denied him. He was also struck by the warmhearted friendliness that members of the Church Army who had come to visit him in the wards invariably showed to him. He was impressed too by their simple Christian faith and by their firm commitment to putting that faith into action in the outside world.

Church Army workers had something of an outpost at the Caterham depot. They had their own base (complete with billiard table), and in this free and easy atmosphere Terry saw Christian witness in action in small but important ways. Church Army men would help out in some of the chaplains' duties, take services, visit families in time of need, and do the hospital visiting. This is where Terry first encountered his colleagues-to-be, and although he had never heard of the organization before, became immensely attracted by the variety of this branch of the Church of England's work.

It was the practical side of it, he was later to say, that appealed to him most, with its emphasis on visible pastoral concern for ordinary people. It might involve running residential homes for the sick and elderly, or setting up emergency hostels for the homeless. Significantly it would involve travel—traveling through the villages, towns, and cities the length of the land.

The Church Army archive reports that it was here that he "felt the first stirrings of vocation." He was now committed to a life of service in the Church, and at this crossroads in his adult life he had to decide on the appropriate direction.

Some time earlier he had considered the monastic life, visiting the Community of the Resurrection in Mirfield, in Yorkshire, but he had come to the conclusion that neither the celibate life nor the ordained ministry were for him. The Church Army was.

In 1958 Terry Waite made the first formal move and went forward to a selection conference where potential recruits were assessed for suitability. The college principal interviewed the young hopefuls, organized visits to various homes and hostels, invited them to speak in public and talk in private to the individuals they met. There were discussions and seminars, questions and tests, but most importantly of all, the selection process was designed to turn the spotlight on the applicant's personal Christian faith. Did its roots go deep; was his attendance at services regular and sincere? What were his real motives for wanting to join up; would his character bear up to the demands of the work? All this was carefully and sensitively put to the test. And Terry along with twenty-three other young men in that year's intake passed. Accordingly the Class of '58 made its way to the Church Army Training College off the Marylebone Road in central London, where two years of study and training were about to begin.

Gordon Kitney (or, to give him his full title, Captain Gordon Kitney, because all Church Army people have ranks) is now a very senior figure in the organization, but in 1958 he was a trainee, one year into the course, and very much in awe of the new recruit fresh from the Guards. In those days recruits from the services were always a pleasure because they arrived with a bit of maturity about them. Many of the recruits had been converted at Billy Graham evangelistic crusades and were rather raw in their faith. "Not that we minded the Billy Graham people one little bit," says Gordon Kitney, "we try to steer a middle course and we're open to everybody, but many of them didn't have the church background behind them. What Terry brought was a great familiarity with church tradition. And it was very refreshing." Well in advance of his actual arrival, rumors were circulating about this impressive man named Terry Waite.

In comparison with our own day, the late fifties were an age of austerity, and college life was decidedly short on whatever luxuries there were around. The colleges of the day frequently modeled themselves on the monastic traditions, and rooms were equipped with the bare minimum of personal effects. The typical study/bedroom was a very spartan affair with nothing more than a gas space heater, a bookcase, a chest of drawers, table, chair, closet, and bed. Television and stereo systems were almost literally unthinkable.

It was a life of order and discipline, with every hour of the day accounted for. Those who were suspected of lighting their heaters to dress or to pray by were frowned on somewhat. Not really "holy" enough, recalls Gordon Kitney. Training officers did a morning round, discouraging this self-indulgent practice!

The early morning bell rang at 6:30. After washing and shaving each would be responsible for making the bed—with military precision—and tidying the room until it was nearly spotless. Morning prayers were at half past seven, breakfast at eight. This was a meal taken in silence in order to train the men (and the women, who ate separately) not to be distracted from the demands of the day ahead. Trying to signal that you wanted a piece of bread, a pinch of salt, or a pat of butter required an elaborate mime show that could produce, as Gordon Kitney remembers, comical moments that had to be suppressed if you weren't to get black looks from your teachers.

After breakfast, twenty minutes long, no more, it was back to the rooms for half-an-hour of meditation and Bible reading. Then the day began!

The evening routine was just as sparse. There was silence from ten in the evening until nine in the morning. In other words, once lights went out at ten you were left to your own personal study and devotions until the period of Bible study the following morning. True, from time to time the rules were subject to "personal interpretation" and a flashlight might just be used to get around the lights-out rule. A highly developed network of note-passing also bypassed the no-talking rule, but in general the regulations were accepted by the young recruits.

Terry's immediate problem was the size of the bed. Accommodating a six-foot seven-inch frame in a standard issue bed is not easy (nor pleasant). Asking for a bigger one, though, might just smack of luxury or self-indulgence, so he had to work out a form of request appropriate to his surroundings. He decided on a verse from Isaiah: "The bed is too short for him which sleepeth upon it." The charm paid off and the matron duly dispatched a bed large enough to take the whole of the Waite body.

Men and women recruits were scrupulously kept apart. Entrance to the college was through separate doors; in classes men were arranged at the front and women at the back to avoid distractions (who might be distracting whom was never explained at the time!); and study quarters were firmly divided off by means of the so-called "Iron Curtain" hanging from a rail in the middle of the corridor on every floor. Separation went so far as to stipulate that should any Church Army man be traveling on a bus when a Church Army sister gets on board, the man must get off. Despite it all Gordon Kitney still maintains that Terry and others were able to bend the "no communication" regulation by leaving discreet notes in the pages of library books that were borrowed by men and women alike.

Lectures in the morning, study periods in the evening, and parish work two days a week, meant that only on Monday afternoon was there any scheduled time for recreation—football or cricket in Regent's

Park. There was occasionally the opportunity to "go out on the town," but with only the equivalent of a couple of pounds a week pocket money from the college such opportunities were severely restricted. One of Terry's contemporaries, David Beardshaw, however, remembers Terry's marvelous sense of economy. "He became supremely adept at nosing out free entertainment," he says. The two of them made an unlikely couple walking down the Edgware Road with just a few pence in their pockets, ready to make an impact on metropolitan life. At five foot three inches tall David (now a vicar in Coventry) provided a stark contrast to his twenty-year-old companion. Their habit of wearing bowler hats and carrying closed umbrellas while Terry walked on the sidewalk and David in the road can only be described as eccentric. Life at the college was clearly not ALL seriousness!

A good way of getting the most out of the meager allowance was to make frequent trips home for short breaks—to stock up on a few basic things and to get a bit of a break from the college routine. Terry was often a guest at David's family home outside Sheffield, and his mother fondly remembered the time when she crept upstairs to Terry's room to drape an eiderdown over his feet which were—of course—protruding from the end of the bed. But if that was noteworthy enough, another habit of Terry's at the time deserves a mention. "He had the habit of darting off on a whim at a moment's notice," says David. "Once when he was at our house he said to me, 'I wonder if there's been any mail at home. I'll just nip back and see.' Now 'nipping back' meant traveling miles and more to Cheshire. But up he got and off he set hitchhiking there and back to be with us again for tea time. Rather strange, isn't it?''

Terry mixed well with his fellow students, but even then Gordon Kitney was beginning to notice the solitary, more reflective side to his nature. "He made friends very easily," he recalls, "but there were always moments when he seemed to want to go off on his own and think things through. He'd always gotten on fine with people during his mission work, but he would frequently take himself off on long walks across London—into churches, into the British Museum studying biblical archaeology or what have you.

"He took a great interest in what was happening in the world at large, particularly in Africa, and was always homing in on places where there was suffering or unrest in the world. He would always be taking off to read by himself—not because he was unsociable, far from it, but simply because he needed time with himself. We all recognized that he needed space and quiet times to reflect on things." It was a quality that his first employer, the Bishop of Bristol, was later to define as "the quality of being able to look inward in order to look outward."

A man of action. A man of reflection.

Life off the Marylebone Road in those days had its lighter moments too, and many of these were at Terry's own lodgings in the Church Army annex away from the main college premises. His room was above a pub, The Walworth Arms, but in contrast to The Ship where his confirmation classes had taken place much earlier, there was no jollity filtering up from the public bar. During his time there the pub remained firmly shut. And the reason for this strange phenomenon paints an interesting picture of the religious climate (and public attitudes) of the time.

The area was the center of considerable church activity. Mission work on the streets, loyal "high church" attendance in the neighborhood, and the strong presence of both The Salvation Army and The Church Army (each with a well established tradition of temperance) brought pressure to bear on the landlord of The Yorkshire Stingo, a pub nearby. In anticipation of the imminent closure of The Stingo it was decided to open another, The Walworth Arms. But it was destined never to open. The religious societies had their way, and the drinkers had to go elsewhere. So any noisy good humor that could be heard from time to time coming from somewhere above The Walworth Arms came not from the regulars in the public bar but from the friends of Terry Waite enjoying singalongs around the piano and impromptu suppers of beans on toast. More elaborate cuisine—in the form of fry-ups—could be produced once Terry had realized that the electric space heater, if turned on its back, could act as quite a useful (and potentially lethal) electric stove.

Terry's brother was an occasional visitor to the London flat in those days. He remembers it as "very studenty" and always guaranteed to produce a lavish welcome. "Whatever was served up, whether it was cheese on toast or sausage and mash, was always served up with great relish and flair," David says. "I know it sounds rather silly, but Terry used to put so much effort into everything that it seemed we were at a banquet."

Visitors to Hyde Park at that time might also have been able to get a glimpse of Terry Waite—not because he was casually strolling through it but because, as part of the Church Army training, recruits were expected to make their way there for a peculiarly English ritual. The idea was that they should not be overwhelmed by public speaking (after all, they might find themselves delivering sermons later in their lives), so practice at this stage was useful. And practice was to be had at Speakers' Corner on the northeastern edge of the park. Open then as now to everyone who wants to deliver a speech, put the world straight, or merely get an opinion off his chest, Speakers' Corner embodies the British right to free speech. And the Church Army put it to good use.

Recruits were expected to go along armed with their obligatory soapbox, mount it and address the crowd. Not an easy task when confronting a demanding audience who had seen it all before. Doubly difficult when trying to get the Christian message across to total strangers who had more pressing things on their mind. The idea was to go along in groups and attempt to attract a crowd. Terry's group had a particularly effective way of doing so, thanks to the sheer terror of one of their number. The recruit in question regularly fainted at the prospect of talking to the assembly, so as a group of people milled around trying to revive the poor man, someone else got up on the soapbox and was assured of a ready-made audience.

Terry acquired an enviable reputation for holding an audience, and was already showing signs of the public speaking skills that some thirty years later could still impress people at Lyneham air base. According to Gordon Kitney he would stand there "like the statue of Lord Nelson" and use a commanding presence to demand attention.

Across the way from Hyde Park Corner was the Odeon, Marble Arch, which proved to be the spur for many an improvised sermon. *Cat on a Hot Tin Roof*, a popular film at the time, might be used for example to illustrate the uncomfortable nature of sin in God's world. It was important for the young men to be able to use the everyday and the commonplace to get across the Christian message, and using the ordinary language of ordinary people was the best way to do that. The experience was also a form of character building. Standing on a soapbox is a very lonely experience—thrilling when the words are flowing and the audience is listening, but uncomfortable when your words are making no impact on a clearly bored crowd. The one way to liven up the proceedings was to throw an egg or a tomato, of course, but history does not record whether Terry Waite was on the receiving end!

Forays into public speaking were followed by forays into public houses, distributing the *Church Army Gazette* and collecting for charity. Contemporary reports say that Terry Waite managed to fill his tin quite quickly, thanks to his ready banter and genuine feeling for the people he spoke to.

There were the so-called "fishing trips" along the Edgware Road; that is to say, evangelizing in groups of two or three and inviting people along to Sunday worship at their headquarters. If a local landlord was friendly there might be hymn-singing in a pub. That particular approach was typical in that it refused to confine worship to a Sunday service in church. Worship could take place wherever people were gathered, and any location was appropriate if the intention behind it was to serve the Lord. Gordon Kitney has fond memories of one such pub in North London where a resident jazz band provided the music.

Contemporaries recall that Terry had the common touch. He could relate to all sorts of people from all walks of life. A small incident described by Gordon Kitney illustrates the point: "We were playing cricket in the park one day," he says, "and after a few moments I became aware that one of our team was missing from the field." No prizes for guessing who that might be. "I looked around and saw Terry sitting on a park bench next to a tramp. He had just got talking to the man in a simple friendly sort of way and was completely oblivious to the fact that the opposition was scoring fours left, right and center. But that was Terry. Always ready to share a word with someone in need."

Concern for people. It is a quality that time and again friends and colleagues, clergy and lay folk have noticed immediately about Terry Waite. "He would never think ill of someone," says Gordon, "never do or even think anything to hurt someone. At college there'd be the usual sort of mischief and so on. You'd go back to your room and find someone had put a bar of blackface soap in your toiletry bag or something. But Terry wouldn't have approved of that. He wasn't at all easy with practical jokes and found himself impatient—even sometimes downright annoyed—with the kind of humor that was hurtful to people."

The great strength of the Church Army in those days was that it had a broad appeal. Students of all sorts of church backgrounds were attracted to it, and the organization was large-hearted enough to welcome them all. Even so, there could be tension. "Some of the new intake had come over from the

Church of Ireland—an intensely conservative branch of Anglicanism," says Gordon, "and they couldn't understand the likes of Terry and me who tended towards 'high church' worship. They used to push all kinds of tracts through our door, thinking somehow we were Roman Catholic. There'd be others from the evangelical end who couldn't believe we were really Christian unless we could stand up and declare that on such and such a day we were converted."

That was precisely the opposite outlook from Terry's. He has taken a more relaxed but no less committed view of his own faith. For him church unity does not mean sinking one's differences overnight into a common pool; it does not mean abandoning one's own dearly held traditions in order to merge into some unrecognizable mass. What church unity does mean for him is mutual understanding and openness, tolerance of differences, cooperation between traditions, and good will among denominations who, all in their different ways, have something to offer to enrich us all. And how do you begin to achieve that aim? First and foremost by being safe and at home within your own faith.

And here it is fair to suggest that Terry Waite provides the model, a model that was already becoming apparent to the young men who were training alongside him.

His love of travel, seen in this light, becomes no longer a mere indulgence. It is an opportunity for experiencing different cultures at close range without ever losing hold of his own; a way of understanding the richness of God's creation and the differences that go into making us all one.

Over the years, as he has grown gently and confidently into his own faith, Terry has learned to feel at ease with others who may express that faith in different ways. Not only that, he has said having one's own deep faith gives one no grounds for feeling afraid of other people's faiths. In this way travel can truly broaden the mind and deepen one's understanding of God's purpose in the world.

It was during this training period for the Church Army that Terry got his first real taste of travel. And to get the precise flavor of that experience it is necessary to imagine oneself back in a world that has long since disappeared. It was barely more than thirty years ago but it has the character of ancient history.

We are talking now not of transatlantic travel, of intercontinental flights, and executive jets. We are talking of the Church Army Trek—a month-long summer mission around the country, with nothing more elaborate than a two-wheel cart loaded up with camping gear, and pulled by a team of half a dozen or so eager young men. Let Gordon Kitney explain:

"Once a year the students would do what was called their summer work. They would set off from a cathedral town and walk from village to village, their cart stuffed full of their belongings. At each stop they would knock on doors, distribute leaflets, organize events, and help as much as they could in the local parish. In the evening there would be a mission service open to all, and in the morning there would be a final service before the team took to the road again.

"Conditions were pretty basic. More often than not you'd find yourself sleeping in a drafty church hall, you'd find your bedding had been gnawed by mice when you got back, and you'd frequently stay overnight in villages where there was no proper plumbing—just water from the well. Bathing would involve several trips to the pump and a delicate operation of shoe-horning parts of your person into the church hall sink. It was all part of the discipline and the fun. Terry enjoyed it immensely."

The summer treks culminated in beach missions at seaside towns like Margate, Shanklin or Cleethorpes, which would mark an end to the two-hundred-mile trail. It seems an age away. But compare the relative dates and you will see that it is not. While Terry Waite was training for the Church Army, John Lennon was studying at Liverpool College of Art—both of them poised to witness the dawning of an age less innocent than the last. The *Robin* comic, sister paper to the *Eagle*, organized seasonal entertainment on the beaches of seaside towns. Joining them further along the sand came the Church Army officers unloading their cart and setting up shop in friendly rivalry nearby. Both might have had puppet theaters and Punch and Judy shows, games and competitions, but the Church Army lads had a message that they hoped would endure long after the summer holidays had ended. The summer beach missions were to be gentle, responsible introductions to the Christian faith in an age when video games and amusement arcades had not yet gained their full hold on our waking lives. Times have changed.

But even in those days there was a general feeling in the air that one era was about to give way to another. The quaintly titled "York Van" was probably the old era's last parting shot. It also served as Terry's first posting once he had been commissioned. The idea was that a group of officers would use a camper

as a semi-permanent base in the York area. It could
be towed around from place to place to enable the
men to help out in a variety of ways in and around
the local parishes. Not half so glamorous as the work
Terry would eventually be doing, but for a young and
eager Christian soldier not a bad first step.

"A mover and a rover" are the words Terry once
used to describe himself. The York Van was fit proof
of that description. Ordination was not appropriate
for him because of his unwillingness to be tied to any
one spot.

Following his father's advice he was well aware
that if he took on a job he would have to stick at it.
Becoming a priest and in turn becoming attached to
a parish would mean sticking not only at the job but
with the parish. And, restless as ever, Terry had no
inclination to be tied down.

But there was another reason for remaining unor-
dained, which went beyond the merely personal. As
a matter of principle he felt that the Church's ministry should involve laypeople as much as clergy. All
too often there was the feeling in a parish that the
vicar was the only one who could do things, and
Terry, like many people, felt that this was an inade-
quate picture of the possibilities for ministry within
the Church. Not only that, a dog collar could often
distance you from ordinary people, who tended to
put you on a pedestal and treat you as somebody
special. He had no wish to see that happen to him.
In fact, dressed as they were in their light gray uni-
forms, many officers knocked on doors only to be
taken as readers from the gas company and shown
the meter!

The work he and his fellow officers were doing

involved helping out with the pastoral work of a parish—doing the rounds of hospitals, schools, private homes and so on—much the same as they had done on weekend stopovers with the trek cart but with a greater sense of purpose and seriousness. It was also a kind of orientation period to allow them to get a flavor of the kind of Christian service most suited to them. There certainly was variety. On one occasion Terry was asked to help out in the cemetery. It so happened that a grave needed to be dug for a forthcoming burial and the gravedigger was unavailable. The Church Army team volunteered and duly set about the task. The problem was that they had come without a tape measure and were at a loss to estimate the customary six feet. At this point call for Terry Waite, pop him in the hole, let him protrude seven inches above ground (that they could easily calculate) and you have your six-foot hole! Needless to say the work was generally of a rather more demanding nature than this.

"A lot of people think Terry's ordained," says Gordon Kitney, "but even when I was training with him he'd made the decision to remain a layman. I would never describe him as ambitious in the usual sense. But he is ambitious on behalf of other people. He desperately wants laypeople to communicate their faith. And he's anxious to bring people who are normally outside the Church into what he calls 'a living fellowship.' He has the vision of the Church as the fellowship of all believers. There's nothing particularly new as it stands, it's as old as the gospels themselves, but he put so much effort and enthusiasm into making the vision a reality.

"He was also aware that a lot of the work done

with the laypeople of a parish involved the younger or middle-aged members, and that somehow the elderly got overlooked. And in just the same way that he could appeal to the very young so he could appeal to the very old. He had a great understanding of the quality of prayer the elderly could offer, and consequently, he spent a great deal of time talking to them and making them feel an integral part of parish life. He appreciated the fact that older people couldn't always take part in the more strenuous activities such as visiting the sick—but equally he was fully aware of the prayer support they could offer to the parish. That rich interior life was an invaluable commodity in the work of the Church but one easily overlooked in a busy parish. Terry took that very seriously."

And here, once again, Terry Waite's dual personality emerges. A man dashing about the parish, busy organizing things, always on the move; but a man with a great capacity for stillness and for appreciating the inner life of prayer, which all his fellow Christians are capable of sharing.

A sense of the inner life and of the need to embark on an inner journey—though that journey could be a painful one—was undoubtedly one of the qualities that got him through his four-and-a-half-year ordeal. "I remember sitting with Terry during our training days," says Gordon Kitney, "listening to a sermon on the Gethsemane experience. It was a sermon that moved us both very deeply. The simplicity of it all. Christ going away from his disciples and saying, 'Father, Thy will not mine be done.' It's that motivation that leads Terry on. He's very conscious in all he does that he is there to do his Father's will."

Toward the end of 1963 an advertisement appeared in the *Church Army Quarterly*. The then Bishop of Bristol, Oliver Tomkins, was looking for someone to organize the training of laypeople in the diocese. Terry Waite was recommended for the post and accepted. It was now that his unique qualities were to be developed to the fullest as he embarked on his first significant posting and began to lay the groundwork for the achievements of his mature years.

Before he arrived in Bristol, however, a rather important event took place. He was married. He met Helen Frances Watters during training days, but engagement and marriage came as something of a surprise to Gordon Kitney. "Terry and I were always thought of as confirmed bachelors in our college days. We threw ourselves into our religious vocation, dashing off here and there, and sinking so much of our energies into programs and projects that people didn't think either of us would have time to settle down. But I suppose we all settle down sooner or later, and it was with Frances that Terry fell in love and with Frances that he settled down."

But "settling down" is a tricky phrase to use in connection with the energetic Mr. Waite.

"When I first met him he'd only been married for two weeks," says his friend and mentor Laurence Reading, "and there we were about to set off for a two-week course in Geneva!" This first real taste of the international life-style he was later to make his own was a long way from Margate and Cleethorpes, a long way from the campers and the trek cart. He was suddenly thrown into the rarefied air of international church politics. The Ecumenical Institute in Geneva attracted scores of church leaders from all over the world, assembling wise and experienced representatives to discuss the weighty topic of "mission" and how best to promote it among all the different denominations. "And in the middle of all this," says Laurence Reading, "here's young Terry! A mere lad, in a way, and only just married."

He had already impressed people in Bristol with his great charm—a mixture of boyish enthusiasm and startling maturity—and now he continued to make a similar impact on foreign representatives. But to be taking part in a high-profile international gathering such as this was something rather special, even by Waite standards. "One of his characteristics," says Laurence Reading, "was to walk in where nobody else would go. To seize quite unself-consciously on some simple point that people might have been too intense to notice. Then he would raise it directly with them. Like a child asking straightforward questions of an adult who is then forced to admit he's baffled, Terry brought this quality of directness to all he did. He had no foreign languages but somehow he managed to establish a relationship with people of different countries and cultures. And he would actually get up and speak in this great gathering where there were really some very able and influential people."

Maybe he had learned more than he would have expected from those days with the soapbox at Speakers' Corner.

Laurence and Terry got along as soon as they met. "I was old enough to be his father," he says, and indeed something of the father/son relationship still survives, even now that Terry is a father himself with four grown children. Laurence, like many others, had really hoped Terry would not return to Lebanon on that last mission, and he like others shared personally in the pain of all those years.

Laurence Reading is a central point of reference for understanding the Waite personality. In some ways the two were similar, with the older man instinctively understanding the younger. The tenderness that grew up between them was as much a product of their genuine fondness for each other as it was a result of their close professional cooperation. The two shared a similar outlook. On paper, Laurence was responsible for adult education in the church and officially had his base at the Church of England's headquarters in Church House, near the Houses of Parliament. But, like Terry, he was not inclined to sit behind a desk all day and lose sight of his goals beneath a mountain of bureaucracy. He too wanted room to maneuver and to travel, to set up plans himself and oversee them personally.

The immediate focus of Terry Waite's attention was a project that the Bishop of Bristol was anxious to see get off the ground. It was a project known as SALT, standing for "Stewardship and Laity Training" in the jargon of the day. Although well-intentioned it had the potential for being the sort of worthy but rather dull church enterprise that is destined to fizzle out quite quickly and to leave no trace behind. This was not to be the case in Bristol where, as people remember, Terry Waite had a not inconsiderable role to play.

Certainly the ideas behind it were extremely important for those who wanted the Christian faith to mean something more than just Sunday attendance and the occasional appearance at the Harvest Supper and Christmas Bazaar. They were concerned with stewardship in the Gospel sense. The scheme was about giving money, of course, but it went deeper than that. It was about giving one's time, giving one's talents, giving one's efforts to the Christian adventure. Above all it was an attempt to get the laity—the ordinary people of a parish—to take a full and active part in the life of the church and to show that that life went beyond the confines of the church itself.

It was vital for the Bishop to appoint a layman to the job or the whole enterprise would seem to be a contradiction—lay training run by the clergy being on a par with Alcoholics Anonymous run by a bartender. Bishop Tomkins had heard good reports of Captain Terry Waite in York and elsewhere, and was immediately impressed when he interviewed him for the job. Enthusiasm and wisdom (an unlikely word for so young a man) are two of the words he has since used when singling out Terry's qualities. But more than that he *liked* the man.

Warmth of personality, an easy manner with people, concern for individuals, tenacity, and above all an overriding commitment to his Christian faith; these were the young captain's most visible attributes. There were, to be sure, many others with such characteristics, and one of their own they were unlikely to cast him into a heroic mold. A rare combination of events would be needed to activate this particular quality. He would have to wait a few more years for that.

4

Home and Abroad

Basil Moss groaned a little when he was told he was to have an assistant. And an assistant from the Church Army at that. The associations were with beach missions and banners, tracts and pamphlets—not to everybody's liking. And not immediately to Basil Moss's: "You see, you had a slot for Church Army people who were just commissioned and assigned to your parish. They came along in their uniform with a known tradition behind them, and although I valued them very highly in certain areas of work, the idea of having one of them as your sidekick was sometimes hard to swallow. The average Church Army officer was rather green, rather evangelical, a bit heavy-handed; and it was hard for me not to get rather impatient with the way they could operate. I respect the movement very much, but in the average parish system if you had to have an assistant the list of priorities went as follows: If you can't have a curate have a deaconess, and if you can't have a deaconess then you'll have to put up with a Church Army captain!

"But I have to say," he added, "Terry shattered that image."

He may have arrived as an unknown quantity but pretty soon he had endeared himself to those he met—as the Bishop of Bristol had a feeling he might. "In Basil Moss," he recalled, "we already had someone working on the stewardship side of the movement. What we were looking for was someone with sufficient theological expertise to be able to conduct study groups and a program of education, and yet at the same time someone who, because he didn't wear a dog collar, could establish himself as one layman talking to another."

The parish of Aston Gate in Bedminster, one of the suburbs of Bristol, had a population of some six thousand people in those days. John Wilson was its priest. His appraisal of the effect of the young Terry Waite on the life of his parish is illuminating: "This part of Bristol was a very densely populated area and one that was dominated by the Wills Cigarette and Cigar factory. That's where most of the work was. Now it so happened that most of those attending the church were employed at the factory. In their day-to-day lives they didn't carry a great deal of responsibility at work, and that meant that they were reluctant to assume any at church. Having a say in things simply wasn't part of their experience, so they'd no reason to believe they could be in charge of anything anywhere—least of all in the church where the vicar ran the show.

"And that's where Terry's help was so important. He played a part in encouraging people to see that ministry was not just the priestly ministry but the ministry of the whole body of Christ."

There was nothing terribly new about the theory behind such a remark. What was nothing short of revolutionary in that part of Bristol at the time was that someone was actually putting that theory into practice. Terry does not take sole credit for that, of course, but he was there when it was happening. And he was part of a winning team—able even now to be remembered with affection by the men and women of the area where he first began to make his mark.

It was not, according to John Wilson, a simple case of running courses in how to be a church warden or how to become a member of the church council. No, it went much deeper than that. "He just came along and talked to people," he recalls, "and believe me, that was new in those days! He would meet different groups to persuade them that they did have potential and that they should unlock it in some way. In those days we were beginning to understand the importance of meeting in small groups outside Sunday worship, to study the Bible or to study some of the moral, social, and religious issues of the day. It may not have been true of other parishes but it was certainly true of areas like mine that there were very few people, if any, who would want or feel competent to lead new programs.

"I remember with dismay, I think after Terry's initial visit, that a particular plan had been suggested involving the congregation itself taking the initiative. At the council meeting, though, they said to me, 'Oh, it would be so much easier if you took care of it, vicar. You're trained to do this sort of thing.' That was the kind of mentality we were up against and it was deeply ingrained. But as a result of Terry coming along and encouraging folk to lead groups themselves, people gradually began to realize they had a role to play. And beside that, of course, it was helping them to see the relevance of the Gospel message in their everyday lives.

"Let me give you an example. We had a couple here who had not been regular attenders but they started to come because they wanted to get married. Now it so happened that one of my curates had preached a sermon basing it on the prophet Amos. It was only when they'd heard it that they began to see that there was a connection between what you heard in church on Sunday and what happened in the outside world during the rest of the week. Now, transplant that into the parish of twenty some years ago and you've got a perfect idea of the attitudes Terry was dealing with at the time. He used to tell them that the Church isn't simply a ghetto for people who are 'so inclined' to meet every now and again. No, the Church is the salt (to use the term that was fashionable then) to add flavor to the rest of life outside it."

Assessing the success of this sort of work is not easy. Not least because it is largely invisible and when things are going well nobody feels inclined to comment on it. They expect things to be running smoothly. But, as far as the Bristol diocese was concerned, everybody is united in thinking that Terry's personality contributed immeasurably to whatever impact this radical new approach was making.

"When I first came here," says John Wilson, "I was really rather disheartened by what I saw. But then Terry appeared, if you like, as a gift from God! I remember one of the church council saying what a delightful man we had here, hoping he would be coming back, and how he cut an attractive figure in our area. It's often said that prophets are without honor in their own country. It's the same too with clergy. People wouldn't take from a parish priest what they'd take from Terry."

But if charm has been a feature of the man's operational strategy, so too has independence. He was affiliated with the Church Army but working effectively for a parish; he was assigned a particular task within that parish but he was not tied down to it. Within a certain boundary he was free to do as he pleased. And that independence has always given him an enviable freedom to move about. But, then as now, independence did not mean distance. His closeness to and warmth for the institutional church have never been in question, as Elizabeth Ralph, a historian and retired city archivist who took a prominent role in church life remembers: "He has never despised the institution and never worked outside it. He may have spotted some of the weaknesses within it and done his bit to correct them, but he's been perfectly happy working right at the heart of it."

In fact someone wanting to work outside the church structure does not join the Church Army in the first place.

A word needs to be said, though, about one "liberty" he was inclined to take. It concerned his uniform. As an officer he was expected to wear the army's distinctive gray. This was no problem when he was a young anonymous captain working in a parish in Bristol, but it became a potential handicap when he began his work as a church envoy.

A rank, a uniform, and a connection with an

"army" could all too easily be misunderstood by governments and factions in the Middle East, for whom Church Army could be taken to mean church militia—giving quite the wrong impression. As a result, and somewhat to Gordon Kitney's irritation, Terry Waite, who should be the best known, is actually the least known officer the Church Army has. Any "uniform" the church envoy has worn—in Iran and in Libya—has been of the ecclesiastical variety. The long red cassock which he sported in Teheran, for instance, was extremely useful in persuading the authorities there of his purely religious status. In a landscape dotted with mullahs and ayatollahs in their clerical garb he was able to fit in very well.

But we digress. In Bristol his career was moving ahead at a rapid pace, even if it was in an area of endeavor less high-profile than that which was to characterize his later success. Running residential courses and weekend seminars for the laity, does not, it is true, have the same aura of glamour that a humanitarian rescue mission to Iran was later to carry, but in its own particular way the work was no less important for all that. It was persuading the ordinary people in a diocese that Christianity matters, that Christianity is a practical system that can be used by everyone to enhance their everyday lives. The weekend courses were giving responsibility to individuals—sometimes for the first time in their lives. Terry was steering them and was always ready with down-to-earth advice. "Don't forget to bring your speeches to a close by half past nine," he once told a seminar chairwoman.

"Why?" she asked.

"So everybody can have time to nip off to the pub

before the evening's out," came the unexpected but invaluable reply.

If residential training courses in themselves were not new, the style of them was. And throughout them all Terry Waite was performing a role he eventually developed with such distinction—that of the mediator. He acted as a bridge between the clergy and the laity, and brought the best out of both. The radical new style he brought to the groups had first begun in America, where the latest science of "group dynamics" was all the rage. "T-Groups" (T for training) were the practical result of the scientific theory. To their great surprise, occasional annoyance, but ultimate satisfaction, the people of Bristol became the guinea pigs as Terry Waite put the T-group sessions into startling effect. This was the procedure:

A course was arranged for the clergy by Terry. It could be a week-long affair, with old hands at this sort of thing knowing full well what to expect from it all. They could not have been more mistaken. They arrived expecting the usual format—lectures, discussions, consultation sessions and the like; a written agenda, and a chairman to steer the proceedings in between lunch, tea, and supper—very straightforward. But Terry had other plans.

On day one the clergy troop in and take their seats in front of the table where Terry sits. They are silent. The silence continues. And continues. A few coughs punctuate the silence but no one speaks. More silence. The clergy are expecting Terry to make the first move and say something, because after all he is the one organizing it all. Terry sits back, entirely relaxed as he surveys the room, and says nothing. Well, by now the tension is mounting and somebody has to say something. "Right—then, we're all here are we? We may as well start."

"Yes," says Terry, "ready when you are." There is yet more silence.

"Look, I've got better things to be doing," says one, "than fooling about like this."

"Come on," says another, "I didn't give up my week for this sort of play-acting."

Gradually a sort of conversation (and not always an amicable one) breaks out, and raises questions from the floor that would normally have been on the traditional agenda. But of course there is no agenda. The participants are working out for themselves what the real agenda is and doing so in the most natural way possible.

The task of orchestrating the "dynamics" took time and was not to everyone's taste. But gradually the mood changed from one of annoyance to one of acceptance. By the second day people were fed up with it. And only the calming influence of a local vicar kept some of the people there at all. By Wednesday the mood had changed. People were suddenly enjoying the freedom of expression, and talking enthusiastically and openly about what really mattered. By the last day of the course they were converts to the technique and were looking forward to the next opportunity for putting all this into practice yet again. Terry was at the heart of it and yet they had done all the work.

His role was that of observer and participant fused into one. He would gently prod the timid into speaking, and just as gently dissuade the over-confident from hogging the show. Then at the end he would try to summarize how the group had performed, pointing out who had agreed with whom for the sake of peace, and who had said nothing at all and been content to let others do the talking.

The end result was that people began to realize how decisions actually get made, and how sometimes a small and unrepresentative group can push those decisions through. It brought the clergy face to face with the realities of their own decision-making procedures. They saw how ordinary folk could easily be excluded from having a real say in matters when large groups of people put their collective mind to it. They saw how easy it was to disagree with what was going on and yet be powerless to influence events. This was the purpose of the T-groups and they had enormous practical side effects.

Canon Raymond Harris, twenty-eight years a priest in Swindon, remembers the impact vividly: "They were totally unstructured groups so that what did emerge was a structure all the more durable for not being structured in the first place. And you could relate what went on at them to the sort of things that regularly happened at meetings in your own parish. Most clergy, if they were honest, would admit they hogged the show. The parson preached a sermon and left it at that. Handing out a spoonful of medicine, as it were, instead of letting the congregation have a hand in its own well-being.

"Let's say you had an important matter to discuss with your parish at an AGM. Perhaps you were wanting to alter the form of worship, or organize a youth club, or let young people use your immaculate church hall to rehearse a play. Whatever the subject up for discussion might be, it was generally felt that the clergy ruled the roost. The vicar would surround himself with a small army of yes-men, prime up the undecided, and by drawing up the agenda and the terms of the discussion in advance, make jolly sure he got what he wanted."

They are observations familiar enough to many a parish priest accustomed to hearing the post mortems after the PCC meetings. How many times had he heard people muttering that they had not got what they wanted, and criticizing themselves for having kept so quiet?

The T-groups, when they were carried out with the laity, were designed to give power and responsibility to ordinary people. The effect of this new discovery was bracing. People were encouraged to use the position of chairman not to rule the proceedings but to offer service to the parish. They would encourage the shy, keep a rein on the domineering, and, yes, silence the boring. But the training sessions were demanding and not always for the fainthearted. Some pretty direct remarks were made and not always politely.

Raymond Harris has particular reason to recall them: "My brother-in-law, who was also a priest, was at one of them. Now, he's a very quiet, reserved sort of chap. After some minutes of the preliminary silence and a few sporadic bursts of discontent, one vicar stood up and gestured toward him with the words, "Well, come on, why don't you help us out? You've been quiet all this time. Why don't you say something?" At which point my brother-in-law, normally a timid sort, barked back, "I'm not saying much because for the moment I've got nothing to say. But I'll say this. You're getting on my nerves. So why don't you sit down and shut up." So all these sessions were very revealing of the basic aggravation that is within all of us. There were lighter moments at the pub but the sessions themselves could get very intense indeed. And when things were getting too heavy Terry would intervene gently and prevent someone from actually walking out."

The whole process was extremely revealing of the underlying attitudes of the day. All too often the new and inexperienced vicar might arrive in a parish feeling the need to show everyone from the start who was in control. What these radical techniques were designed to demonstrate was how much more he might be able to achieve by withdrawing from the action and letting others decide. It was a means of unlocking individual potential for the benefit of all. Many of the clergy came out of the sessions invigorated, prepared to bring new energies to their ministry, and equipped to avoid the kind of unpleasantness and misunderstanding which might have dogged it in the past.

The simple and often painful question they were being asked was whether Christian service or empire building was at the heart of their work. Raymond Harris expresses it theologically: "If we truly believe that God accepts us as we are and that we belong to Him as children then we have to express that joyful brotherhood in our lives. When someone new comes into the Church we have to convey our utmost concern for the newcomer and welcome him in with open arms. Unwittingly, we as a church keep newcomers at arm's length. These courses in what you might call 'self-awareness' helped us to understand the barriers we were putting up between ourselves and the laity. I mean, I can remember spending two hours or so in meetings deciding what kind of broom to issue the cleaner. Two hours! And why was that? The answer is that up until that point they had never known how decisions were made. Up until that point if a festivity was to be organized they were told a festivity was to be organized; if a mission was to be launched they were told a mission was to be launched, and they did what the vicar told them. When it came to brooms well, for once, they knew a bit about those so they could get in there and get excited about matters. Now they could influence events! The whole point of the training was to cash in on that sort of enthusiasm and make ordinary contributions count for something in parish life."

That is where Terry Waite came in, as someone enabling people to take charge of their own lives after half a lifetime of being told by others how to organize it.

If the work sounded unremittingly intense the man behind it was not. He was prized above all for his good humor and sense of fun. One year, for example, the annual Bristol clergy conference was scheduled to take place at Butlin's Holiday Camp in Minehead. Some of the more staid members of the clergy were heard to emit distinct groans of misgiving at the prospect of spending a week in (horror of horrors) a holiday camp. The Bishop was wise enough to suspect this might be the general reaction so he sent a letter to everyone concerned.

"At the time of your ordination," he wrote, "you promised to obey your bishop in all things lawful and honest. I cannot see anything unlawful or dishonest in my requiring you to come to Butlin's Holiday Camp."

It is at this point that Terry comes into his own. In the first year of settling into Bristol, Frances had twins, and by the time of the Minehead episode the two girls, Ruth and Clare, were toddlers. The whole family went along, and although Terry was only an observer he was soon to be seen taking the lead in the fun, leaping into the pool with the children, and generally contributing to the relaxed feeling of gaiety. His infectious sense of humor was transmitted to everybody, and the course was all the more successful for it.

Throughout this period he was proving to the Bishop that he was the right man for the job. On paper that job was simple enough: to equip ordinary people to be articulate and well-informed leaders of local Christian communities. But in practice it meant putting a tremendous amount of energy into overcoming apathy and indifference, an energy that only the truly dedicated could summon. Terry Waite was the man to summon it, his energy apparently limitless. He was able not only to communicate with people but also to associate with them, to enter into their lives and see things from their point of view.

Such a precious quality was later to help him enormously when dealing with people of different faiths, nationalities, and political systems. He could see the problems as they saw them, not simply as the West saw them. He might condemn hostage-taking and disapprove of hostage takers, but the desperation that led people to take hostages in the first place was something he was prepared to understand. That comprehension (so often ruled out by Western leaders who felt that to understand was to encourage) did not amount to approval. On the contrary, his ability to see things from the other person's point of view made his disapproval all the stronger and gave him an extra degree of bargaining power.

Terry of course enjoyed the challenges of the work immensely. His status as layman ensured that he was not seen as a threat to people. A clergyman involving himself in the training programs of another clergyman's parish might have been regarded as "butting in" on someone else's territory. A layman—especially one with the charm of Terry Waite—was no such threat. It all worked smoothly.

But it was in Bristol that a major disruption upset the smooth running of things. His father had fallen ill, lung cancer had been diagnosed, and he was given only six months to live. "The six months came and went, and eventually turned into eighteen," says Terry's brother, David. "For me, and I'm sure for Terry, every day that did come would see me asking myself whether it would be today that my father would die."

The strain was drawn out and Terry would make regular trips from Bristol to see his father. In the final months the two of them became closer than they had ever been—something which David says gave their father enormous comfort. He recalls that Terry kept his emotions deep within him rather than show his sorrow publicly.

Terry was twenty-eight when his father died. Sadly, he was not able to be present. He had telephoned his mother to say that he had a preaching engagement one particular week, and asked whether he should cancel it in order to travel north. His mother said there was no need since the condition of his father had not changed over the past days. Unexpectedly, however, it took a turn for the worse.

Lena contacted Terry in Bristol. He came immediately, but when he arrived at midnight his father was already dead. Although it upset him greatly he was able to keep his emotion (publicly at least) in check. He conducted part of his father's funeral, and impressed his brother by his bearing at the service and by the great sensitivity he brought to a traumatic family event.

In private prayer and public worship it was clear that Terry was (and is) a deeply devout man. Elizabeth Ralph is not alone in remarking that the authority he generates is not one which comes from the job he does but from a spiritual source much deeper than that: "You feel that Terry carries an inner authority. One not bestowed on him by earthly powers or even by the Church, but directly by God himself. I remember saying to the Bishop once that he really does seem to be a man whom God is using."

Laurence Reading confirms the view: "It's a kind of childlike quality, really, which somehow gets through to other people. It's an almost Franciscan attitude he brings to things. This man really does believe! He isn't an evangelist in the strict sense, not a proselytizer; he just embodies the faith, letting it infuse everything he does."

Very shortly this characteristic was to be exported.

He had been chosen as part of an international team from England, America, and Africa to conduct training courses for the bishops and senior clergy of Uganda. By now he had mastered the art and craft of the psychological T-group training methods and incorporated them into his whole approach.

The ideal would be to leave in every parish an

inner group of committed laypeople who knew each other, trusted each other, and were dedicating whatever gifts they had to the service of God and their fellow men and women. This was the essence of the stewardship principle that they tried to lift from the Bible and to graft into the everyday experience of ordinary people. By their example they would be a beacon for others. They would embody the Christian ideal and demonstrate its abiding power for good in a fallen world.

The work Terry and his colleagues carried out in Bristol may seem small scale in the context of the high-profile work with which he was later to be involved, but its impact was every bit as significant. It was nothing short of an attempt to transform the lives of men and women and fill them with the vision and commitment of the early Church. So what of lasting impact did Terry Waite achieve? Raymonds suggests an answer: "The real changes he brought about were in people's ways of thinking. Anybody can make superficial changes and think they have done a lot. It doesn't take much real talent to build an annex to the church, to rearrange the seating or to plan a new church hall. But to alter the time-hallowed ways in which people behave, to allow them to see ahead with a clearer vision, now that, to my mind, is real and lasting achievement we can all be proud of."

In 1969, with such thoughts uppermost in his mind, Terry Waite and his family set off for a new challenge. They left Bristol behind and set off for Africa, where Terry had accepted a three-year contract as a lay trainer to serve the needs of the developing church in Uganda. It was at this moment that his globe-trotting really began; and from this moment that events began to come together in a way that provided the setting for one Christian's particular greatness.

That was not, however, in immediate evidence when he first set foot on African soil. Terry Waite arrived in Uganda with a bang, and made headline news in *The Uganda Argus* on the day after his plane touched down. Philip Turner, however, initially wished things otherwise. He stared down in horror and disbelief at the front-page story. Mr. Turner, chairman of the Uganda lay training board that had just hired Terry Waite, took more than a moment to adjust his eyes to the shock. There was Terry caught by the newspaper photographers' cameras holding two smaller men by the scruff of the neck.

"Oh, my goodness," Turner thought, "what have we let ourselves in for? I took one look at the picture and couldn't believe my eyes. Here was this huge great white man collaring these two guys like some colonialist arriving in foreign parts to take charge. If this was how things were going to start, where would they eventually lead? What hope did we have for success in the mission work? I was aghast."

He need not have worried. Indeed, as he read on, the matter became clearer. Within a couple of hours of his arrival Terry had been caught up in a robbery. Two men had tried to steal a car and Terry had decided to intervene. The paper portrayed him as the hero of the hour—a strong man fearlessly stepping in to uphold the forces of law and order. Philip Turner is incredulous even now: "I always knew he was the sort of person to get right in the middle of things, but to get himself on the front page of the paper within twenty-four hours, well, that was really something."

Life calmed down a little in successive days, but the initial impact of Terry's arrival impressed itself on the people with whom he was later to work. He was always a bit theatrical, perhaps; larger than life, certainly; but difficult to ignore and impossible not to admire. Terry Waite's hour, many must surely have felt, would soon be coming.

5

Active Service

The church in Uganda at that time was going through a critical phase. Those privileged to work for it could take a share in the glory it was eventually to attain. Terry's first visit there had been to develop leadership and organization within the church, and it was while attending a conference there that he and Philip Turner first met.

"I liked him immediately," Philip remembers. "In fact I pushed hard to get him taken on here permanently. We actually met in the Mulago Hospital where a friend of mine had come down with appendicitis. As we walked through the ward I was straightaway taken by his directness. I had him marked down as a very canny man who would have no difficulty working with all sorts of people."

The project he was running at the time—forming a nucleus of specialist training staff able to be deployed at short notice throughout the country—was funded by the Church of England's sister organization in America, the Episcopal Church of the United

States. Many people thought at the time that because there was American money involved an American should be chosen to run it. Philip Turner, an American himself, was not so sure, and saw in Terry Waite the ideal candidate. He persuaded the authorities and Terry was selected.

The training program was not exclusively an Anglican operation, and from the start it was envisaged that the Roman Catholic Church would be involved. Not for the first time—far away from the sometimes restricting conditions of the British system—could the two historic churches sink their doctrinal differences to allow men and women of good faith to work together in God's service.

This particular brand of religious cooperation was tailor-made for Terry Waite. "He took to the job immediately," says Philip Turner, "and had a wide vision of what it should entail. From the outset he knew we needed to involve the Roman Catholics."

There had, however, been a long history of division between them and the Church of Uganda, and Terry Waite was not alone in realizing that if lasting progress was to be made, then contact at an official level should be established. Fences needed to be rebuilt, cooperation needed to be re-established. This was where the Waite touch came into its own, as he was careful to build Roman Catholics into the program from the very start. There was a further reason why the two churches should work together. They were the only two bodies of any size that had the organizational structures stretching into practically every village in the land.

In many ways the attitudes they encountered in Uganda were no different from those operating in

Bristol: the villagers they met expected outsiders to do the work and solve whatever problems they had. Not because they were incapable of doing the work themselves but because somehow they lacked the self-confidence. Philip and Terry named this "The Million Shilling Syndrome." By this they meant that people invariably felt that the ability to change things did not lie in their hands. Only with outside resources—millions of Ugandan shillings—could the troubles be overcome.

When the team of trainers arrived in a village they would hear a long catalog of problems. Perhaps the water supply was poor, perhaps a new school needed to be established. Many a time the people were almost paralyzed into inactivity because they felt deprived of outside resources. This was where the new techniques came into action and where the real work began.

The trainers embarked upon long and careful discussions with the villagers and drew from them—exactly as had happened in Bristol—a picture of what individual talent the community could rely on. Could they not get someone to provide wood for a school building, could they not pool resources for books, could they not draw on one another's goodwill to achieve something modest for themselves rather than wait for something grand from someone else?

To mobilize the corporate will meant changing the way decisions were generally made. In the past, village or tribal elders would decide what needed to be done and tell everyone else to get on with it. The only way villagers could express their objections was by doing nothing. And so nothing was done. When the team arrived, the first task was to put these ancient and accepted patterns of leadership under scrutiny so that ordinary people could be encouraged to have a stake in their future.

"What Terry and I were trying to do," says Philip Turner, "was to harness human and financial resources. It was a case of getting things done by getting people to know that they could do them. And in this Terry had enormous natural ability."

When the Waites flew out (now with a third young member of the family, Gillian) they stayed first with the Rev. and Mrs. Eric Hutchison of the University of Makarere. Later they moved on and settled at Mukono, the theological college where Eric, a Canadian, worked. His wife, Elspeth, remembers a fresh-faced (and beardless) Terry Waite, friendly and full of jokes, and given to striding into a room with a twin daughter on each shoulder. With twins of her own she remembers a house full of shrieking youngsters.

Left in charge of the Waite brood, often for lengthy periods, was Terry's wife, Frances. "She has deep reserves of hidden strength," Elspeth Hutchison says. "I don't think many people have appreciated that."

But perhaps, in the four years and more of her husband's absence, people finally did realize it. She conducted herself with great dignity under increasing fire from the media. Her chosen strategy of emotional survival was to decline all comment and interview. In that way she avoided swinging needlessly between the twin poles of optimism and despair. She bore her suffering in silence and devoted herself to keeping the family in good spirits during the long years of her husband's captivity.

Between the periods of separation in Uganda, when work would take Terry off for days on end, life went on against the glorious backdrop of the hilltop at Namirembe ("the place of peace"). The family had moved here to a modern house next to the cathedral. Guavas, paw-paws, pineapple, mangoes, and bananas grew in profusion together with exotic flowers of every possible shade and hue. Despite the delightful setting, life subsided into a routine like any other.

A car pool was drawn up to take the children to school and back. Terry was often to be seen at the wheel of a sturdy Peugeot estate, with a full load of screeching boys and girls behind him, entertaining them with a repertoire of jokes and stories.

For the rest of the day there was no shortage of things to do. Walks around the hill, prayer meetings and shared suppers, trips into the surrounding countryside, simple family pleasures. Despite his long absences Terry Waite is always thought of as a family man. Some friends have felt resentful on Frances' behalf that she has had to endure countless days apart from him looking after the children alone in foreign parts. But equally, friends have referred to the time they spend together as "quality time," important for its intensity if not for its duration. Terry himself is aware of the hardship that they have had to suffer when he has been away, and he has referred to the family in the past as "a pretty tough group."

All are agreed that it was from his secure family life that Terry drew comfort and strength for what, even then, could be hazardous work.

Though the training groups were, in essence, those of the Bristol years, the circumstances were often far more demanding. For one thing they were trying to reverse the pattern that had established itself over generations. In the past the tendency had been for the African to defer to the European, and for the European to set the agenda. Now the missionary team was prepared to learn from the local people, and to harness their own particular qualities for shared Christian service.

The "group dynamics" sessions could be tricky. If not properly supervised they could also be quite destructive. When people were given the green light to say what was on their mind, some pretty uncomfortable things could be said. As a result an experienced trainer needed to be on hand in the event of individuals feeling pushed beyond their endurance. It was very easy for the darker side of human personality to emerge on occasions like these, and sessions had to be conducted with great care.

Despite the risks there was great benefit to be derived from the groups. They enabled people to put into practice in a very direct way some of the Christian virtues of forbearance and forgiveness. When people did get angry they became reliant on the group to offer its forgiveness and they felt immeasurably grateful for it.

"In many ways," says Elspeth Hutchison, "the profound Christian concepts of penitence, atonement and resurrection came alive in gatherings like these. The results were creative in the end—not destructive."

The period was crucial for the church because it was a period of transition. Up until this point it had been run totally by white clergy. Although Terry Waite was an advisor to the first black archbishop, Erica Sabiti, the official structures were by and large white-dominated. Here was the opportunity—if strong local leadership could be established—for the balance to shift, and for a complete handover to be made. They were exciting times and Terry was happy to be taking part in the pioneering venture.

"It was an attempt to see people much more on the footing of equality," says Eric Hutchison, "an attempt to view things from the African perspective." And who better than Terry Waite to be prepared to stand in another man's shoes, to gauge the experience from exactly where someone else was standing?

The deference that Africans traditionally displayed to Europeans at the time could mask deep division and disagreement. Terry and the team were not prepared to accept things at their face value. They wanted to get below the surface in order to discuss the things that really mattered. A common phrase Laurence Reading and Terry used in their time together was "What's actually happening here?" In other words, Terry and others were interested in the strategies people employed to reveal or conceal what they were really feeling. They were, if you like, games people were unwittingly playing with each other.

And if people were playing games then the trainers used games to achieve their own ends. Which partly explains what a group of Roman Catholic nuns were doing, under Terry's supervision, slapping each other on the legs with rolled up newspapers! But we shall leave that for later.

Terry's careful and tolerant approach to people and to alien cultures was clearly emerging too. His refusal to make judgments about people's ways of life meant he was more readily accepted into a new community. On matters that seemed to fly in the face of the Christian ideal he learned to keep wise counsel. For example although it was dying out, polygamy was still practiced in parts of the country. This would often survive even when Christianity had been embraced (although curiously enough, only the first wife was allowed to join the Mothers' Union!). Rather than raise his hands in horror and condemn the practice at a stroke, he was content, if asked, to gently say that lifelong monogamy was the true Christian way. More than that he would not add, out of respect for local differences and so as not to insult people whose traditions could not be changed overnight.

In short, Terry was prepared to accept people as they were, not as they ought to be. And when invited to attend Mothers' Union meetings he politely addressed them all—knowing full well that for every woman present in the cathedral three or four were standing outside excluded from the proceedings.

He was careful to familiarize himself with local custom, and to pass on the fruits of his learning to aid agencies that needed to know how best to help. He might say to UNESCO, for example, that dried milk was acceptable to the Baganda tribe but that egg powder was not—eggs being associated in their minds with infertility.

The unwary could fall into traps. As did Lena Waite—though it has to be said not catastrophically—when she went to Kampala on a three-month visit to see her son. She too had been invited by the Mothers' Union to talk about domestic life in Britain, and had been called on to give an impromptu cooking class. She returned home to tell Terry of the day's events, only to relay to him that she had demonstrated the art of scrambling eggs. The look on Terry's face is not recorded although Lena herself insists the ladies there enjoyed the results.

Laurence Reading remembers how Terry relished the local customs. One year he flew out to Entebbe to see him, and was met at the airport by Terry and Philip Turner. There was much to talk about. It had, after all, been some time since the two of them had worked closely together in Bristol. Before the conversation got underway Terry suggested that they all sit beneath a big tree in the African way.

"That was the traditional way to do things," says Laurence Reading with great affection, "so that's how Terry did them. He excelled at that sort of thing and it was all great fun. That was his style, enjoying life but never taking it lightly."

It is something borne out by his former employer, the Bishop of Bristol: "He clearly understood that to be a good Christian layman didn't primarily mean being busy. Rather it meant having depth, and unless you had spiritual roots and made time for quiet all your activity would be futile."

Here is the paradox of the Waite personality. It lies in the apparently perfect balance of the active and the contemplative. People who had watched him jet from trouble spot to trouble spot beneath the glare of television lights may not always have appreciated his capacity for stillness, but if they needed any proof it was surely in the measured speech he delivered at RAF Lyneham during his first few hours of freedom. How could a man have survived such an ordeal and emerged from it so graciously if he had not had the ability to look inward, deep into himself, and rely in the stillness of his heart upon God, the Sustainer of all life?

But to return to Uganda. The hilltop walks through the bougainvillea were losing some of their charm in the late sixties, when events were brewing that would eventually boil over into the coup in 1971, which saw Idi Amin take power from Milton Obote and open up yet another troubled chapter of suffering in the country's already troubled history.

The first signs of lawlessness were the cars stolen (often at gunpoint) in the city center. Terry Waite himself had two cars stolen this way—the second from outside his house close by the cathedral. It was at this time that he mounted a series of nightly patrols in the mission compound to check that the single missionaries there felt secure.

There were other troubles in the region too. A civil war had been raging for over a decade in Sudan, and casualties from the south were streaming over the border into the country creating a huge refugee problem. A group of men and women regularly met to coordinate medical relief efforts to the southern Sudanese but they had only limited success. Measles, smallpox, cholera, and sleeping sickness were ravaging the country, and what small efforts were being made to fight the diseases were being hopelessly undermined by the continuing war. If emergency aid was important, peace was vital.

In the effort to find some sort of solution to the political and social grievances that were separating the two sides, and in a desperate attempt to stop the bloodshed and the human misery, the World Council of Churches decided to intervene. A mission was duly dispatched to the north to investigate the chances of mediation.

What most concerned observers was that contact with the south had been largely overlooked, and it was felt that nothing positive could come out of any mediations if only one side took part. It was vital to persuade the WCC representatives to see the southerners. How to do this? That was the question.

Dr. Louise Pirouet, a lecturer in religious studies at the time, was also an active member of the Sudan emergency relief team that had initially responded to the effects of the crisis. Terry Waite, a fellow member, was helping others to address the causes. The reasoning went as follows: If the Archbishop of Uganda, who was head of a member church of the council, could be persuaded to invite the delegates from the WCC down to Uganda (and they could barely refuse) then the prospects of both sides meeting on neutral ground, with independent mediators present, could give peace a healthy chance of survival.

Many people were ultimately involved in the eventual negotiations that led to a peace accord in 1972, but in Dr. Pirouet's view Terry Waite's intervention was crucial. He had the confidence of the Archbishop and knew how the mechanisms of the WCC operated.

In the end, representatives were persuaded to come to Uganda to meet all the players in the drama, and peace was eventually declared. Terry was now working with others on a much wider international stage than his previous largely localized endeavors had involved. Dr. Pirouet was impressed: "He was sensible and wise. One had the sense that he didn't act rashly but that he could act fast."

There is no doubt though that he rather enjoyed it all: the excitement, the involvement, and, yes, the personal thrill of adventure. But is a climber any less brave for enjoying the exhilaration of the climb, is he any less courageous for being inevitably drawn to danger?

In Terry Waite's case his personal satisfaction (which has occasionally been at the service of a not inconsiderable ego) has been chiefly at the service of his Christian faith. The commandment has been to worship his Father in heaven and to help his fellow men and women on earth. If in doing the second part of that great commission he has found his true vocation, then surely we must applaud. Those cast in the heroic mold are rarely as we might expect them to be. To repeat, we must take them as they are or not at all.

On the day of the coup in Uganda an event occurred that typifies this. There had been shooting around Kampala, and a friend of Louise Pirouet, a friend whose husband was away in Nairobi, was left alone in the house. "We were all worried about her," she remembers, "because she was not what you would call a practical person, and we weren't quite sure how she would react in an emergency. It was quite easy for me to see her by slipping round the hedges on the hill where we lived. So l went to check up on her and of course Terry had to be there, didn't he? He had driven right across the city in his Peugeot car. He was quite cheerful and I suspect he half enjoyed it." One might take issue with the "half"!

It is tempting to see in the element of risk that Terry so relished an allegory of faith itself. Trust involves risk. Guarantees of certainty, safety, and success would make trust redundant. Why bother to embark on the adventure of faith if watertight guarantees are handed over at the outset? We have to trust that all shall be well without expecting it to be so.

"I remember Terry saying to me," says Louise Pirouet, "that unless one behaved openly and honestly there could be no way forward, and that sometimes one had to risk it to make any headway at all. I remember him repeating it much later in England: that sooner or later you have to trust someone. That's the risk, isn't it?"

Throughout the peculiar circumstances of these lawless times Terry was learning skills never taught by the Church Army Training College. They were skills picked up as part of the continuing experience of living life on the edge of things.

"If you're involved in some sort of risky operation then you have to learn to keep your mouth shut," says Dr. Pirouet bluntly. "We all learned that in Uganda. If you're in a hotel you learn to sit where there's so much music that you can't be overheard. You look around to see if anyone is listening. You don't tell anybody anything." The result of that attitude, if prolonged, can be a degree of solitude. It might go some way toward explaining one aspect of the Waite temperament, toward explaining how the solitary and the gregarious can coexist in one man.

His enjoyment of life looks set to become legendary. Foreign corespondents will testify to his great good humor in times of danger, his coolness under fire, and his healthy appetite for food and wine.

At some distance from the excitement of Beirut, Louise Pirouet can corroborate that assessment. Just as she has seen him in danger in Uganda so she has seen Terry Waite summoning his traditional zest for life on social occasions with friends. No meal with Terry, she says, is eaten without other diners turning around to see where the laughter is coming from. His seriousness and his levity are perfectly matched.

———

His time in Uganda was now coming to an end. The three-year term was complete and in that time Terry had learned much. His period of training was now well behind him, his probationary term in Bristol had been an immense success, and his experience of Christian service abroad had taken him swiftly into the mature phase of his career.

He had had a taste of responsibility and it agreed with him. The known boundaries of a provincial clerical life were not for Terry (though he would never devalue the incalculable contribution those attracted to it could make). No, that was not his style. He was "a rover, a mover." That was, quite simply, the way the good Lord had made him.

His time in Africa had brought him into frequent contact with the Roman Catholic Church, at its official and unofficial level. Many of the Catholic missionary societies recognized in him—an Anglican—a great resource, a great Christian resource. For them it was a time of great change. The Second Vatican Council, which had sought to bring the church face-to-face with the modern world and to breathe a spirit of renewal into all aspects of its life, was beginning to have an impact on the visible church at every level. Accordingly the religious houses were undergoing profound organization and it was something of a shock to the corporate system. Terry was seen as the ideal person to help reorganize their structures.

What he was doing, of course, was nothing of the sort. He was too experienced a practitioner to fall for that one. What he was in effect doing was helping them to help themselves reorganize their own structures.

So it was that the Waite family set off yet again

for a foreign shore. This time they were bound for Europe and for Rome, where Terry was to take up his appointment as advisor to the Roman Catholic Church.

The Peugeot had by now been exchanged for a Volkswagen, which was filled to capacity as the family drove off to Mombasa. A most important piece of "luggage" had been inserted at the last minute: a small wicker basket containing the latest addition to the household—a young son, Mark, delivered by Terry himself some months earlier, and far too young to appreciate what new experiences lay ahead for him and the whole family as they cut their links with one continent and prepared to settle in another.

By way of a holiday they sailed around Africa for a month before docking in an uncomfortably cold winter in Spain. A boat took them on to Trieste and a plane brought them finally to Rome. Terry Waite had planned to stay for two years but ended up staying there for almost seven.

6

A New Departure

*T*he Medical Mission Sisters were Terry's new employers; an international community of trained and qualified doctors, nurses, pharmacists, and hospital administrators who had chosen the religious life. Sister Jane Gates, their American Superior General, was his official boss.

For the children, there were minor adjustments to be made to come to terms with the luxuries of the Western world. The elevator, for example, that took them to their apartment in a five-story building in central Rome was a novelty undreamed of in Uganda. As was the sensation of being several floors off the ground. But the greatest marvel of all was the television set—a secondhand, black-and-white affair that worked a near hypnotic effect on the three girls.

"They never took their eyes off that set," says Sister Jane, "from the moment Terry walked in with it. He balanced it on the table and the girls took their seats on the three solitary dining chairs and sat in a row glued to this wondrous machine. If they got up

93

to walk out of the room they walked backward so as not to miss a moment." But by far the strangest phenomenon the younger members of the family now had to confront was of quite a different order from the elevator, the flushing toilets, and the TV.

On their first evening Sister Jane took the family back to supper at the communal house. As Mark dozed contentedly in a laundry basket, the girls were full of questions. There was something odd about the place and they could not think what it was. Then it dawned on them:

"Daddy, why are there no men here?" ventured one. "Why are there no other daddies like you?"

Terry attempted an explanation but Sister Jane recalls with some amusement that it somehow failed to satisfy them. There were no further questions, so there the matter rested.

Back at their own apartment, life settled into a familiar pattern of warm domesticity. The sisters provided furniture for the new arrivals, and helped find a school for the girls. St. George's, which the children attended during their stay in Rome, was an English school (complete with the traditional English educational system) transplanted to the heart of the Italian capital.

A further English touch was supplied by Terry himself. "Normal" Italian cars, he concluded, were too small to accommodate his ample frame. The solution was to import a London taxi. That way he could have a small compartment to himself and enough space at the back to load children and luggage in endless quantities. The familiar black cab and the familiar beaming bearded figure at the wheel now became permanent features of the small cosmopolitan community that the family had joined.

The flat now served as Terry's operational base. It was from here that he planned his foreign trips to a bewildering number of countries. The Medical Mission Sisters had houses in the Philippines, Indonesia, Pakistan, Bangladesh, Ethiopia, Kenya, Uganda, Malawi, South Africa, Swaziland, Ghana, Latin America, Germany, England, Holland, and the United States. Whether Terry actually got to every single house in every single country is not certain, but he had to be ready to set off for foreign locations at a moment's notice.

And yet even though he was absent from home much of the time, staff in Rome remember him as a family man. "He was a wonderful father," says Sister Jane. "When he was back he would arrange lots of different outings to the park or to the seashore, always treating the time as very precious. I always felt he conveyed to his children the strong feeling that whatever they did was important, that school grades or swimming lessons, or whatever, were things he really cared about."

The time at home was indeed precious. The demands of his work were enormous and required him to be absent for long stretches of time. Typically the job he had secured was one not easily defined. Yes, he had been hired as an employee of a mission society, but what precisely that employee was assigned to do remained unclear. Terry Waite himself defined his role. Working within a basic framework laid down by the sisters he alone was responsible for drawing up the content and the style of his training programs.

What has characterized the man from the very

earliest times is his capacity for self-motivation, his ability to be his own man. And his tendency to spring surprises!

Sister Jane had first met Terry in Uganda where the by now legendary "group dynamics" were deployed in one of the society's mission hospitals. She remembers vividly the shock: "He had given us all rolled-up newspapers and instructed us to whack each other on the back of the legs. I think the point was to discover what kind of anger or irritation he could produce, and what the limits of our own tolerance were. Every now and again he would call out, 'You're not hitting hard enough. Really give them a good hard whack!' Meanwhile he sat back enjoying it all enormously and quaking with laughter at our inability to hurt one another!"

The spectacle of a congregation of nuns, sleeves rolled up and armed with folded copies of the *Uganda Argus*, trying to whack each other about the calves, may not suggest missionary work of great seriousness. But that is to miss the point.

Following the Second Vatican Council the Roman Catholic societies and institutions of all kinds felt the need to reorganize themselves. Their aims, objectives, structures, administration—everything was undergoing a radical reappraisal. In the past they had been part of a highly authoritarian system with superiors and subjects. If people needed something the first step was always to ask the Mother Superior. There seemed to be a general paralysis of initiative and will. Individuals had been schooled not to think things through for themselves but to rely on others to do the thinking for them.

After the renewal meetings in 1967 the sisters

were expected to negotiate among themselves and take control of their own destinies. Having been part of a rigid structure, however, many of them encountered severe difficulties adjusting to the change. Now that the rigid structure on which they had relied was gone many felt vulnerable and insecure. They had to learn how to assert themselves for the first time, and how to negotiate things by themselves instead of by the rule book. It was all very disorientating. And that is where the rolled newspapers came in!

Here was a flippant but effective method of breaking down barriers within the hierarchy. The exercise was relaxed and informal, and so unlike anything the sisters had done before that the old roles of supervisor and supervised no longer applied. It was all very liberating.

There had initially been some surprise expressed that an Anglican had been appointed—and a married man with a family at that—but the authorities had been overwhelmed by Terry's experience and expertise in what was a highly specialized field. The enterprise was given the title "Project Rediscovery" by the sisters themselves, who realized that there was an urgent need for personal and institutional renewal throughout the whole of the Catholic Church if it was to honor the commitments made by Vatican II. Terry Waite's role was to enable them to communicate with each other more effectively as Christian women, and to show them how to share responsibilities as a community.

Jane Gates' successor as Superior General in 1973 was the Dutch sister, Godelieve Prove. She took over at a time when their international meeting, the General Chapter, was scheduled to take place. The meeting provided an opportunity to assess the work done so far and to look forward to the next few years.

By now Terry had worked with them for three years. His work was bearing fruit, giving the society as a whole and the individuals within it greater confidence. It was felt that one more year of his involvement would be sufficient. In that time he would be able to consolidate his achievement, after which he could hand over the reins to the sisters themselves, leaving them in full control of their operations.

Describing the impact he had on the communities' lives is not easy, just as it was not easy to quantify the achievements in Bristol or in Uganda. As one of Terry's friends puts it, "Anything he does is hard to put into words. It's not like a production chart where you can measure success on a graph. It's a never-ending process involving more and more development as a person and greater and greater commitment as a Christian."

To get an impression of his contribution it is instructive to study his impact in one place in particular. In the early '70s Sister Sheila Collins worked in a small mission hospital in Western Kenya. The enormous upheavals of the past few years had ensured that morale was low. Before Vatican II there had been a much more monastic way of life, with a highly structured community life-style. They would work, pray, and eat together, and even had formal (and compulsory) times for recreation. The lines of communication worked from the top downward. There was somebody "in charge" and the rest did her bidding.

The atmosphere was all the more restricting because the set-up (a group of expatriate sisters who kept very much within the boundaries of the hospital and convent) was relatively small. They worked hard, often doing several jobs at a time. As they looked back on their lives and assessed their own personal achievements they felt that their very professionalism as medics, which was the initial reason for their foundation over sixty years ago, was actually a barrier between them and the people they served. As the mission hospital grew, the running of it became more and more complex.

"Bits were being added on here and there," says Sister Sheila, "but the organization of the hospital couldn't keep up, and the lines of communication, which looked simple on paper, ended up extremely complex. When the hospital secretary is also the social worker, and when the pharmacist is also the hospital secretary, the whole organization breaks down. There really was chaos and confusion within the outwardly quite formal structure."

Little wonder morale was low. What the Second Vatican Council provoked was a change in leadership style. Instead of being told what to do sisters were expected to participate in the running of their own houses. But to do that they had to be prepared to cast off years of habit, and that was often a painful and confusing business. At which point, once again, enter Terry Waite.

He would organize groups, sometimes small, sometimes large; sometimes for "leg-whacking," sometimes for serious discussion; sometimes for debate, sometimes for conversation—in short, a mixture of settings where individuals could relate to each other in different ways. Taking a role that did not intrude on the action, he was able to observe what was going on, what games people were playing, and how the articulate were deliberately or inadvertently dominating the reticent. Once the session was over he would report back to them, telling them what he had seen and asking for reaction.

Far from being dry theoretical exercises they had great practical relevance to the work at hand. In the early days of mission the attitude of the European had been to take the dominant role in helping the needy. Local projects were overlooked as the European model was wheeled in. When Terry came along that model was changing, and the emphasis, from then on, was to be on cooperation and partnership in a shared venture.

"What Terry helped us to do," says Sister Sheila, "was to gain confidence to help local staff, from Kenya to the Philippines. To assume leadership, authority and responsibility in our hospitals."

The whole business could seem, at the outset at least, rather threatening, but those who met Terry at the time were soon put at ease, not least because his respect for a religious tradition he himself did not share was evident from the very start. "Appreciative of the positive in people" is how one sister described him. And another: "Everyone was precious to him. From whatever culture or whatever religion, they were important. And he, in turn, saw their infinite potential."

The characteristics had long ago been spotted in Bristol by Basil Moss: "He was supremely happy in a team and anxious to get people to work in teams." But he did not favor traditional teams with a captain and subordinates. No, what he preferred was for everyone to be flexible enough to give and take orders alternately. In the case of the mission houses, this new arrangement could be very hard to accept, so he needed all the sensitivity and powers of persuasion he could summon.

For many of the sisters the reorganization was a crossroads not only in their working life but in their spiritual life as well. For them it represented the most serious challenge to their vocation they had experienced. Terry Waite was well aware of it. To enter convents and mission houses when many women were re-evaluating their most cherished beliefs called for tact and sympathy of a high order.

In Manila, Sister Victorina de la Paz recalls the sensitive encouragement he gave them when he arrived: "Although he was not a priest, he told us how much he valued the life of the religious. 'Stay in,' he said gently but firmly. And his words were of great encouragement to those of us who felt our vocation wavering. His benevolence and his talent for reaching the most traditional of us and the most modern of us were very attractive."

But another quality that won them over was rather odd in a man accustomed to moving in and out of new experiences in foreign places. People noted in him a strange vulnerability. "He always needed lots of reassurance," said one sister. "He would come up to you regularly after a group session and say, 'How did it go? Did it go well?' "

On the evidence of those he trained, things certainly did go well. One of the society's district supervisors, Sister Kathleen Brown, was full of praise: "I admired his ability to stay in the background and keep his mouth shut. And that, among a group of women, is quite difficult, I can tell you. But all the time he was silent he was listening—able to pick out the essential thread that linked all our remarks. The fact that he was an Anglican made no difference. Nor did the fact that he was a man. The Church has been male-dominated for two thousand years. We're used to that!''

Pleasing such an international society was no simple task. The sisters came from different backgrounds and came with different outlooks on the world. Given that it was something of a pioneering society it was also natural that it would attract highly independent-minded individuals. When the society was founded in 1925 by Mother Anna Dengel, religious sisters were forbidden from practicing medicine. She had thought the arrangement unjust and formed the society to provide more opportunities for those who were attracted to medicine and to the religious life.

In her way she had been just as much an innovator as anybody could be. The fact that she was alive when Terry's appointment was made (and apparently happy with it) was the ultimate accolade. "The final seal of approval," says Sister Sheila.

We leave this chapter in Terry Waite's life with the future church envoy standing on his head surrounded by nuns and singing a song at the top of his voice.

———

A word of explanation. First, he had not cracked under the strain. Yes, the work was hard and the hours long but he kept his marbles throughout! So why the "Old Father William" impersonation? The answer was that after long periods working in the mission houses a warm relationship between him and the sisters had invariably grown up and they were always sad to see him leave.

More often than not a party was arranged at which individuals might do a "turn." Terry's party piece involved, for some reason best known to himself, standing on his head and singing a song. What these gatherings proved yet again was the convivial, extrovert side to his nature. Amid the laughter and the song the light side of his personality would bubble uncontrollably to the surface.

"That was Terry all over," says Sister Sheila, "a delight to be with and an important figure in all our lives. He set things in motion for us. Or to choose another image: he sowed the seeds and then we reaped the harvest. We were rediscovering our purpose, rediscovering our vocation. To help us do that was Terry's great mission."

Meanwhile his pioneering work was not going unnoticed by other missionary societies in Rome, who saw in this man not only someone of great ability but also someone with great access to the mission fields abroad. Already he had been described as "the very model of a transcultural person," a man at home within any geographical boundary. The young Terry Waite had dreamed of travel during his childhood in Cheshire, but he surely had not dared to hope for this.

And there was more to come (membership of The Travelers' Club in London has been no coincidence). After his work for the Medical Mission Sisters he looked around for employment and soon found it. The Servizi Documentazione e Studi organization, or SEDOS, as it was known, had good use for a man like him. Here was an umbrella organization serving a number of Roman Catholic missionary societies throughout the world, providing them with information, research material, facts, figures, and statistics to help them in their work. The aim was to avoid endless duplication of documentation piling up in filing cabinets throughout the city. Here at SEDOS was a central resource open to all.

On the face of it, the job was deskbound and full of paperwork. In practice, it involved much travel in order to send back reports of conditions in the field. The value of the information was vital for societies planning mission and development work abroad.

Details such as soil erosion, water supply, local diet, road and rail communications could all be of use to missionary work in distant countries. All these considerations might have important implications for the long-term survival of a church, and gave people advance warning of what missionaries should be prepared to tackle.

More than once the work has been compared with the achievements of the Benedictines in the Middle Ages. They too were developing their wide knowledge of matters great and small, and establishing an international network beyond the confines of their cloisters. All this they pursued alongside a life of prayer and an active social involvement in the world. SEDOS may have had computers where the monasteries had libraries, but the principle remained the same.

It was certainly as an internationalist that he wanted to make his name. There is evidence in letters to friends that he found England too constricting, too parochial, and insufficiently interested in the work he was doing for SEDOS. His contemporaries from the home country seemed similarly unimpressed by his work as a roving consultant on mission work. "I have very little contact with England these days," he wrote rather gloomily to Laurence Reading in 1976, "but it was hard to stimulate any interest in what I was doing in Rome, so I tended to keep away."

All the evidence seems to point to the conclusion that foreign mission agencies valued his work more than English ones. In letters he talks with great enthusiasm of the vast range of projects he is involved with. "I have just returned from the States and the program for the coming year looks interesting," he writes. "In September I am back in the Philippines and India, and late November I am in West Africa." He adds that the next day sees a departure for Sicily—but this time, doubtless to general relief at home, the six-week trip is to be a family holiday.

A couple of years before finally leaving Rome he considered a career back in Britain as a mission director based in London, but at the last minute he withdrew his name from the list of applicants and decided to branch out as a free-lance consultant with his base in Europe.

What eventually persuaded him to return was the question of education for the children. They, if not he, needed stability and continuity. With this in mind the family was on the move again.

Seven years of life and work in probably the busiest and most complex religious capital in the world came to a close. There was just one problem. Terry Waite had no job to go to.

Making your mark on events means being in the right place at just the right moment. To a degree these things can be planned in advance but more usually

they simply happen. The guiding principle for Terry
Waite was that he was there to do God's work and
that in the end the good Lord would provide. In faith
and hope he returned to England.

His first post late in 1978 was of a temporary nature on the Africa desk of the now defunct British
Council of Churches. Staff there remember him as
kind and courteous, and prepared to treat secretaries
as if they were senior clergy. He did not stay long,
becoming increasingly bored by a job that involved
deskbound bureaucracy at the expense of practical
work in the field. It was tolerable work but not guaranteed to provide the long-term satisfaction he
needed. The Waite career was going through a temporary lull. A combination of events, however, was
set to change his career in the not too distant future.

That combination of events waiting to come together was eventually activated by the appointment
of a new Archbishop of Canterbury, Dr. Robert Runcie. Then Bishop of St. Albans, he would soon be
preparing to appoint his personal staff to fill the administrative offices of Lambeth Palace. Dr. Runcie
would be anxious to raise the international profile of
the Anglican Church, and to emphasize its relationship with the other historic churches worldwide.

Such a task was not possible single-handed and
he needed a reliable lieutenant by his side; a man or
woman whose ample experience in world affairs
could be harnessed to serve a relatively new depart-
ment. Colleagues of Dr. Runcie had suggested to him
that he would need someone capable of forging international links with the rest of the Anglican Communion; someone capable of preparing the ground
before a visit, accompanying him and advising him

on his travels, and then following up any developments on his return.

The Archbishop of Canterbury performs, in fact, three jobs rolled into one. First, he is a diocesan bishop, though the Canterbury diocese recognizes that it has comparatively little claim on his time. Secondly, he is Primate of All England, with enough domestic issues to keep him more than occupied. And thirdly, he has to keep his eyes on the international scene as President of the Anglican Communion worldwide. In this last role he badly needed an assistant.

Terry Waite, of course, was the ideal candidate, but at this stage he had no idea that such plans were being drawn up.

By late November 1979 the work he was doing for the BCC was clearly becoming a chore. He needed more stimulating employment and sought the advice of his former boss in Bristol, Oliver Tomkins, who still maintained his links with the church hierarchy. Perhaps he could suggest something.

Little did Terry know at the time that Oliver Tomkins and a colleague, John Howe, were actively sounding out recruits to serve on the staff of the new Archbishop. Bishop Tomkins knew that the expertise Terry had would take years for someone else to acquire. It would have been a pity, he thought, to waste such accumulated experience when it could prove invaluable if harnessed to the Lambeth Palace operation.

John Howe was particularly impressed by Terry's apparent casualness in matters of employment. He was struck by the way in which he had left Rome with no idea of what he was going to do, trusting simply that something would turn up. "Things that would have daunted most people," he says, "didn't bother him at all. He reckoned all would be well in the end."

Neither Bishop Tomkins nor Bishop Howe had any intimation of the greatness within Terry Waite. They both recognized that solid expertise, and global experience (coupled with personal warmth and flair) gave him outstanding qualifications—but for what exactly, no one was quite sure.

Much earlier Basil Moss had put it a different way: "I didn't know where he would end up but I knew he was going somewhere. I would describe him as totally unambitious as far as his own career was concerned. He was an adventurous man always looking for new fields to explore but always harnessing that love of adventure to a real sense of vocation."

In April 1980 an important meeting took place. Appropriately enough it was in Rome, scene of so many of Terry's earlier triumphs. There had been a conference on Uganda held at the Vatican, and Terry had gone along as someone with firsthand knowledge of the country. The two others at the meeting were Canon Sam Van Culin and John Howe.

During a break for lunch the three men sauntered through the city in search of food. They sat down on the terrace of a pavement cafe and ordered. As the food made its way to their table they talked of this and that, with John Howe gradually steering the conversation to Terry's employment prospect and to the possibility of working in some capacity for the new Archbishop.

Now the cat was beginning to emerge from the bag, and for the first time what people had been talking about privately became public knowledge. If—just if—Robert Runcie considered taking on an international advisor, would Terry be interested? His enthusiasm for the idea was instant. He would be very interested indeed.

Armed with this information John Howe could now go to Dr. Runcie and inform him that a possible candidate for the new post was available. Dr. Runcie, of course, needed to meet Terry personally to assess his suitability. Up until that moment he had never even heard of the man. A meeting was arranged.

In the meantime Dr. Runcie was also seeking the opinion of those who had known Terry personally and professionally over the years. Bishop Tomkins' recommendation was crucial. "He has gifts of personal charm," he wrote to the archbishop designate, "which seem to guide him through many ticklish situations, combined with a soundness of judgment that is unusual in a comparatively young man. He knows how to work gently and slowly but with a firm sense of overall direction. He is physically tough enough to travel continuously, and with a wife and family who have come to terms with it completely, I think. This was well tested in Uganda, and the confidence of the Roman Catholic authorities in his work must be considerable for they have no wish to lose him. He is a convinced Anglican, all the surer for his close appreciation of and admiration for the Roman Catholic Church. He already has good ecumenical links in Geneva and elsewhere . . . [and] . . . we should be wasting a very gifted son of the church if we can't find a position that fully stretches him as an interpreter of Anglicanism." When Dr. Runcie read that, the rest was a mere formality. The job was his.

Not that Terry Waite dominated the press head-lines or got himself into the public consciousness from day one. In the early days it was a very different job from the one it later became. On paper he was simply the Archbishop of Canterbury's Secretary for Anglican Communion Affairs. Not a hint as yet of the "special envoy" status. There was much going and coming across the Thames between Lambeth Palace and the headquarters of the Anglican Consultative Council, the administrative heart of British Angli-canism. Interesting work, solid, challenging in its way, but . . . how shall we say . . . headline-grabbing. Iran was to change all that.

By now Dr. Runcie was beginning to appreciate the qualities of the new man. The energy and the ability were not passing by unnoticed. Sure, he en-joyed moments of wry amusement as he observed the very buoyant Terry popping his head around the var-ious office doors keeping an avuncular eye on things and checking that everything was "all right."

Were there perhaps echoes here of the lay trainer dashing from seminar to seminar asking, as he had of the Medical Mission Sisters in Uganda, "How did it go? Did it go well?"

He was gradually making the job his own. Just as the sisters had an overall plan for him to carry out within which he was free to operate as he saw fit, so the requirements of the Lambeth Palace post left him considerable freedom to move about. To that degree Terry has always been something of a free-lance op-erator, a sort of ecclesiastical troubleshooter with no precise job description to his name.

Besides that he has been very much an Establish-ment figure too, enjoying employment within the very traditional structures first of the Church Army, then of the Roman Catholic Church, and now of the Church of England. Neat in blue suit and tie, perhaps making his way to his gentleman's club on Pall Mall, he looked the very model of a sober civil servant mandarin. In short, a walking contradiction defying all existing categories.

That constant tension of opposites is the key feature of the Waite personality. The man of action and the man of contemplation; the family man who is rarely at home; the team player and the solitary individualist; the convivial host and the withdrawn loner.

It was while he was in Uganda that he first began to read the works of the Swiss psychologist, Jung. These were to have a profound effect on his thinking. His colleague, Sam Van Culin, was aware of their importance in his approach to life: "For a thoughtful, sensitive man in his mid to late thirties, living in a variety of cultures and confronted with a variety of religious questions of an emotional and psychological nature, the psychology of Jung affected him in a way other psychologists didn't. For one thing Jung takes religious experience seriously. And Terry takes God very seriously."

Through Jung he found it possible to make sense of apparent contradictions and to see that, deep down, these contradictions could be accommodated and resolved creatively. He has spoken of the Anglican Church, for example, as embodying "passionate coolness" to which he is inevitably drawn. While the words may seem to contradict each other, a man like Terry can live with the contradiction. It expresses his real attachment to something about which he cares deeply, but at the same time it hints at his distance from it.

But this sort of inner reflection is, of course, only half the picture. As he traveled around the world with the Archbishop, arranging his trips, preparing the ground, and briefing him on local matters, he was "action man" personified. And always delightful company, ready to break out into spontaneous laughter at the slightest cause.

On one occasion, for example, he found himself in Africa alongside Dr. Runcie as the two of them attended the enthronement of the present Archbishop of Uganda. Among the guests was an old friend, John Wilson, whom Terry had not seen since his Bristol days. Wilson remembered the meeting well:

"The great thing was that Terry and I just carried on where we had left off twenty years ago. It was so gratifying because, although we hadn't seen each other for all that time, not even been in touch, it was as if we'd been in each other's company just the day before. I'd watched him from afar with great interest but we had never made contact. I remember he was wearing a white cassock, and frequently going up to the Archbishop to have a word while we waited in a line outdoors for the food to be served.

"This attracted the attention of several Ugandans, who made a point of telling me that this big man was the Archbishop's bodyguard. 'You see that large man over there?' they said. 'The reason he's so huge is that he's covered in guns beneath that white cassock of his.' Later as this feast wore on I told him that lots of people here thought he was swathed in arms and armor and, of course, he bellowed with laughter and told me that it happened quite often. The point is that we were able to relax in each other's company immediately and there was no sense of standing on ceremony." Equally the two of them were able to share a huge belly-laugh partly at Terry's expense.

Despite the humor there was real underlying seriousness. On another occasion Elizabeth Ralph remembers him returning fresh from China in readiness for the Archbishop's trip there: "There he was among these high-powered clergy carrying out his job to perfection. And I remember saying to Bishop Oliver [Tomkins] that he really does seem to be a man whom God is using. He himself believed that God was directing him, that things were bound to be all right. And I also remember thinking to myself how wonderful it was that a man like Terry, who had had a limited formal education, could be doing what he was. I mean, it just goes to show that intellectuals are not always the right people for the job."

Dr. Louise Pirouet, herself an academic, agrees: "If you're working under the conditions we were in Uganda, academic qualifications don't come into it. He could have had five degrees or none. I simply didn't ask because it made no difference at all."

Arranging the Archbishop's international trips was interesting work. Within the relatively small world of church bureaucracy it brought Terry a degree of renown. But as far as the British public was concerned Terry Waite was an anonymous figure— greatly loved and admired in ecclesiastical circles, totally unheard of outside them. By December 1980 a series of events in the Middle East was beginning to unfold that would transform Terry's status at a stroke and forever.

This little-known church diplomat would find himself catapulted by force of circumstance to the very heart of one of the greatest national, social, and political upheavals of the late twentieth century.

Terry had not changed but part of the world had— irrevocably. And he was present as history was being made.

Iran had ushered in a new religious and political era. The old order under the Shah had become, for the majority of Iranian citizens, intolerably corrupt and decadent. Western materialism and excess were thought to have corroded the purer ideals of an earlier civilization. Islamic fundamentalism had violently overthrown an equally violent tyranny and was now in control.

The turbulence of the time caught many innocent people in its net. Terry had been dispatched to bring them back to safety. From that moment his life was never to be the same again.

, It was as if all the qualities that had made him what he was could now be deployed in full. With the benefit of hindsight you could say that all his life had been leading up to this point. His moment had arrived.

7

Into the Fire

For the Anglican Bishop of Iran the first sign of real trouble became brutally evident within a week of the change of power in February 1979. His senior priest was murdered in Shiraz. Within a month a group of Islamic "fanatics" who he said much later had been a constant source of trouble for the past twenty years moved in to claim the fruits of newly acquired power. They took church land and seized control of two church hospitals that they now claimed as their own.

Even then there was, according to the Bishop, the Right Rev. Dehqani-Tafti, some semblance of the law and order they had formerly known. They consulted their lawyers and even appealed to Ayatollah Khomeini himself. But without success.

The intimidation from the gang continued. They raided the house and the office, and took away everything from books to photograph albums before setting fire to church files. The Bishop was told to sign a piece of paper. Had he done so he would have released the diocese's trust fund and effectively signed away the church's property. He refused and was taken to the Revolutionary Court in Isfahan where he feared the worst.

The worst was deferred for a few months. In November of the same year a group of armed men burst into his bedroom at dawn. His wife woke up first and saw the gunmen. Since Islam forbids the killing of a man while he is sleeping they roused the Bishop before pointing a gun at his head. His wife threw herself over him. Five shots were fired. After her screams had subsided and she contemplated the blood stains on the pillow, she realized her husband was still alive. Four bullets had circled his head and the blood was from her own hand, which had been the target of the fifth.

They left the country to attend a conference in Cyprus shortly afterward. Behind them they also left the confusion and chaos that was to engulf the three British missionaries whose release from imprisonment Terry was soon to secure. One of them was Jean Waddell, a small, soft-spoken Scottish woman who had earlier been secretary to the Anglican Archbishop in Jerusalem.

When she left in 1976 to take up her new post in Teheran, under Bishop Dehqani-Tafti, one of her friends remarked innocently, "Gosh, won't you find Iran dull after Israel?" There are many words to describe the turmoil of post-revolutionary Iran but "dull" is not one of them. The excitement she (and others) encountered, however, was something they could have quite cheerfully lived without.

The signs of the times were easy to read long before the real violence. The sixty-strong choir made up of singers of all different nationalities had staged a performance of *The Messiah* just before Christmas, to tremendous local reviews. A few weeks later, invited to perform it again to repeat the success, the choir had dwindled down to half a dozen or so, and they were forced to cancel. The reason was simple. As soon as trouble was expected the various societies had withdrawn their people. The Americans in particular were among the first to leave.

Anti-American feelings were at boiling point, with mass demonstrations in the capital protesting at the antics of the country they had dubbed "The Great Satan." Hundred of thousands of people filled the streets. Students chanting, middle-aged men joining in the chorus, and an assortment of mullahs and clerics riding down the main street lent an air of unreality to it all, but the event deeply etched itself on Jean Waddell's mind.

From Cyprus the Bishop had traveled to England where he eventually settled in exile—advised not to return to Iran for fear of his life. Jean Waddell, who had been with him at the conference, did return and noticed that the country seemed to have been transformed overnight.

All signs of the decadent West had been removed or destroyed. There were burned-out shells where cinemas had been, smashed windows where fashion shops had sold the latest French dresses, and empty rooms where cafes and bars had once stood. The whole country now came under the official writ of the clerical ruling class. Islamic fundamentalism was established.

After spending a night under curfew in Teheran, Miss Waddell made her way to Isfahan from where she prepared to transfer the church's offices back to the capital. It was at this point that trouble began for her. On May 1, 1980, she opened the door of her apartment to be confronted by two gunmen. They interrogated her for some time, curious to know why she, a foreigner, was still around. What was she doing here? Who was she working for? Was she spying? Not satisfied with her answers they knocked her out, tied her up, bundled her under an eiderdown, shot her, and left her for dead. They were never to be caught.

As yet there was still some semblance of normality, despite the fact that "fanatics" could burst into a woman's apartment and attempt to murder her in cold blood after first subjecting her to a "trial" where they were judge, jury, and executioner. The police and ambulance were called.

The first thing Jean remembers is the sight of a burly Iranian policeman breaking down the door before taking her to the ambulance and then on to the hospital for emergency surgery. She was comforted by the Bishop's wife, who was shortly to receive tragic news of her own. Her son, Bahram, had been shot dead. It was clearly time for everyone to leave the country.

In August Jean Waddell applied for her exit visa in Teheran but was ordered instead to make her way to Isfahan where she was interrogated again. She was suspected of spying and thrown into jail with no idea of how long she was likely to spend in detention.

In a particularly cruel piece of psychological manipulation she was led to believe that she was the only survivor of the Anglican Church in Teheran. All the other members had either fled or had been executed. It was, she said later, a living nightmare. In an ordeal that was strangely minor to Terry Waite's, she was kept in solitary confinement for months on end and had simply lost contact with the outside world. Her sense of abandonment in the women's wing of the high-security Evin Prison was complete.

Then in December she happened to see an English-language edition of *The Teheran Times* and read that the Archbishop of Canterbury, alarmed at events in Iran, was about to send an envoy to help. Miss Waddell was not the only Anglican to be accused of the absurd (and false) charge of spying. Two British missionaries, Dr. and Mrs. John Coleman, had been similarly detained along with four Anglican priests, who were also Iranian nationals.

Meanwhile, in London, Terry Waite had acquired a new title and a new role. As the Archbishop's "special envoy" he prepared to set out on Christmas Eve on a mercy mission that was to change his life forever. Modern history was in the making and he was in the thick of it.

And what was his role? Simply that of a Christian mediator, not a negotiator. There is an important difference.

The negotiator has something to negotiate with. He has arms, or cash, or the promise of trade links. In short, he has power. The mediator has nothing to offer and comes powerless. All Terry Waite could persuade the Iranians with was his moral authority as a simple man of God. Force of character and the power of goodness was his only armor and his sole defense. He came alone as an independent representative of the Anglican Church, which had mercy as its only bargaining chip.

Shortly after his arrival Terry was able to visit

Miss Waddell at the prison. That first encounter lives with her still: "I was taken down to an interrogation room, escorted by a guard who didn't seem to know herself where we were going. We went up and down stairs and I had no idea what to expect. Then this door opened and there was Terry. He's such a big man, with such a warm comforting presence, and he just clasped me to his bosom."

It was characteristic of the man that his greatest quality at that moment was his presence alone. It was, as Elizabeth Ralph had remarked much earlier, as if God was using him as a channel for His power. The fact that Terry had traveled out simply to *be* there was in its way as important as the mediation work itself. Here in that interrogation room, where two people gathered together in Christ's name, was the Lord's saving Grace.

Very soon the everyday realities of the situation pressed in on them. What was needed now from Terry was that particular blend of shrewdness, charm, and, above all, Christian concern for others.

The Revolutionary Guards had eyed him with great suspicion and had harsh words for him. They quoted the injustices done to them under the old regime, and expressed their hostility toward the corrupt West. And that included the Church. They continued in this way for some time while Terry simply listened. He did not argue back nor strike a confrontational position, he merely listened, absorbing all the hurt into himself, understanding their pain and their grievances and putting himself in their shoes. It was an act of great humility. When the outburst had ended he and the Guards were speaking as friends.

The Anglicans had been the object of some sort of conspiracy aimed at incriminating them. Terry was able to prove that the charges were implausible, but not before persuading them of the rightness of his case by sheer force of character.

He was known by the guards as "the two-meter man," possessed of an impressive physical presence which could easily intimidate. The fact that his calm personality contradicted this initial impression made his impact all the more effective. There were friendly bouts of arm-wrestling as he and the guards spent hours waiting for news. By all accounts they were won over by his boyish charm and the evident sincerity of this faithful servant of the Church.

On February 14, Jean Waddell was told that she was to be released. There was one more psychological twist before she finally emerged into freedom. Expecting to meet Terry Waite immediately, she was instead put into a sealed car, driven to the woods nearby and forced to spend three days in a detention center. Then she was blindfolded, driven into Teheran at midnight, and led into a room.

The blindfold was removed and there beneath a magnificent crystal chandelier stood the other six prisoners. On February 28, she and the Colemans stood by Terry's side on the tarmac at Heathrow. He tried to keep anonymously in the background, but disguising his towering presence was not easy. And, besides, he felt a short speech coming on.

It was a triumphant moment by any standards. Under the glare of the world's media a hitherto unknown churchman had pulled off a feat of great daring, which had succeeded where secular diplomacy might so easily have failed. For its success it relied on establishing a common vocabulary of faith, an appeal to the one true God and to the mercy He radiates. True, the charges had been bogus, but that fact alone might not have been sufficient to gain the prisoners' release. What was ultimately needed was the dimension of trust. And that quality Terry was ideally suited to bring.

His work in Uganda and his travels throughout the world brought him into contact with Islam and, although not sharing it, he could understand it. Secure in his own faith he could respect it. And he spoke as someone familiar with the language of faith, as someone at home with the religious dimension of daily life. It was that understanding that established his credentials as a man of the spirit who, however remotely, had something in common with the men of good faith in Iran at the time.

He also wore his humanitarian heart on his sleeve. He put the value of each of the missionaries' lives at the top of his list of priorities, and remained convinced that, when pressed home with firmness, humility, and integrity, the cause would appeal to the most intransigent of religious zealots.

This was a unique situation. It needed a unique figure. Thus are heroes made.

The press was not far behind with accolades of its own. He became "the Church of England's Dr. Kissinger," specialist in ecclesiastical shuttle diplomacy, or the "miracle-worker," pulling success out of the hat where only failure had seemed possible. When the excitement had died down the image of the man lingered on, and people who found themselves in trouble looked to him for help. It would be difficult, from now on, to refuse. That was the price of success.

In 1984 Carol Russell, at the time totally unknown to Terry Waite, had troubles of her own. Her husband had been working in Libya as an English teacher during a period of extreme political uncertainty. In the late spring of that year there had been an attack on the army barracks. The attack added to the tension in the air, and security measures were tightened by the authorities. In situations of political instability foreign workers are easily caught up in events. In the paranoia that can ensue, Westerners are particularly vulnerable and can find themselves, as Jean Waddell had been, the subject of farfetched allegations.

Such was now the case with Alan Russell, an occasional organist at the Anglican Cathedral in the Libyan capital, Tripoli. He was rounded up for no particular reason and found himself detained with three other expatriate Britons: Malcolm Anderson, an oil engineer; Michael Berdinner, a lecturer; and Robin Plummer, a telephone engineer. The four of them, all strangers to one another, were arrested and jailed. They were to spend the next nine months in detention—though none of them knew at the time of their arrest how long the sentence was to be. Their innocence of any charge was not deemed an important enough reason for clemency.

It was, in fact, Carol Russell's mother who first thought Terry Waite might be able to help. She lost no time in telephoning him, and he agreed to go to their home near Ipswich to talk matters over. He was evidently concerned but spent a long time asking Mrs. Russell questions to prove to himself that Mr. Russell had not been justly imprisoned for breaking the laws of the country. Any suggestion of political involvement would undermine any effort Terry might eventually make on their behalf. Once he was satisfied, he agreed to help.

Mrs. Russell was very impressed and put her total trust in him. "I knew that here was a man who could accomplish something."

This again was the price of success. He now carried the heavy burden of their complete confidence. Whenever the mission seemed to be suffering one of its numerous setbacks, Terry could not allow himself to feel despondent. He knew full well that he had pledged his Christian service to families in need. When they suffered, he suffered too. He had not volunteered his efforts in the first place, had not put advertisements in the newspapers selling his efforts to the highest bidder. No, he had merely responded to a genuine human crisis. He had become involved simply because he had been asked.

But the nature of his mission now subtly changed. In Iran he had been employed on church business. Anglican missionaries had been detained on implausible charges of spying and he was clearly the man to go as a representative of the very church to which the detainees belonged.

Libya was different. The group had only the loosest links with Anglicanism (thanks to Mr. Russell's appearance at the cathedral organ), so the new mission could not be justified in terms of Church of England business. On the other hand, what was Terry Waite to do? Was he to turn down this heartfelt appeal? And was the Archbishop to prevent him from carrying out a Christian duty? Visiting the prisoner in jail—was that not what the gospels commanded?

As a result the mission was justified in terms of its humanitarian appeal. A precedent had been set.

Carol Russell's next move was to contact the families of the other men, who now became intimately bound up in Terry's own future. Their worries would be his. He was straightforward with them from the start. "He told us he would tell us what he could," says Mrs. Russell. "He said he might withhold certain things but that whatever he did tell us would not be a lie. And we all appreciated that."

The political temperature was rising both in England and Libya. Terry Waite was caught up in it all despite his best intentions. As he tried to operate as an independent church mediator, events were happening all around him that made his sensitive position more sensitive still.

The biggest blow came when members of the Libyan People's Bureau holed themselves up in the embassy in St. James' Square in central London, and without the slightest provocation opened fire on unarmed police outside. A young woman police constable, WPC Yvonne Fletcher, was casually murdered on the streets of the capital. Public outrage was at its height. Diplomatic relations were severed, and the Libyans were expelled. Still the innocent men were held in Tripoli, and Terry Waite knew that his mission was going to be under the utmost strain.

He came under fire from people in his own country, too. As he shuttled back and forth, there was no shortage of commentators accusing him of bringing his country and his church into disrepute by shamelessly bargaining with a foreign tyrant whose standards of humanitarian concern had been amply demonstrated to the sound of gunshots on London's streets.

This was a low moment for him. He took the in-

sults with great dignity while continuing to fulfill the
promises he had made to the hostages' families. Be-
lief in the justice of his own cause kept him going.

But at home even his strongest supporters were
privately skeptical that he could establish any sort of
common ground with the unpredictable Colonel
Gaddaffi. As local groups of political representatives
paraded him at various Libyan People's Congresses
in Tripoli it was clear that he had a high propaganda
value and that he could be exploited without any of
his conditions being met.

He had a faithful supporter in the shape of Laurence Reading, who thought he might just have the
necessary qualities for his most delicate task to date:
"It was that innocence again. That determination to
find something in this man that would bring about
some sort of rapport of communication." The appeal
was to be to the common ground between Christianity and Islam, to the common humanity the whole
body of believers could share independently of national or political affiliations.

On one of his visits he took the Colonel a gift, a
scholarly work on the influence of Greek culture on
Arab life in the seventh century. It was a Christmas
present offered to the Libyan leader during a two-
hour meeting in his Bedouin tent on the afternoon of
Christmas Day 1984. They talked about matters both
light and serious. The Libyan leader made a point of
sounding him out throughout the conversation to discover whether his motives were as pure as he had
suggested. Could they be sure he was a church representative pure and simple, or was he perhaps an
agent of the British Government?

Eventually he persuaded them of his good faith.

"Politics are made by men," he was to declare, "justice and mercy are made by God."

It was easy (and not always wrong) to be skeptical. Libya was desperate to restore its credibility to the outside world and to reestablish economic and education ties between itself and Britain. If it could string out the Terry Waite saga long enough and release the prisoners (who were innocent anyway) at a symbolic moment, the country might have gained considerably by this episode and cunningly used it to its own advantage.

Some said as much in the press, accusing Terry Waite of being a foolish innocent at large in an adult's world. Or worse, of debasing himself to appease a cruel dictator. He was in a position from which it was difficult to emerge with credit.

That is not, of course, how the men's families saw things. Aware of the political realities they were also painfully aware of the human dilemma.

Diplomatically the government's hands were tied. Only an independent mediator, caught in the political crossfire and paying a price for it, had any hope of success.

That success relied on establishing a climate of trust between two seemingly irreconcilable systems. Basil Moss, a friend from the Bristol days, was not surprised he could pull it off: "Talking to Gaddaffi was entirely characteristic. On the basis that he believed in God, Terry would have thought it entirely appropriate to give him the credit for some sort of integrity and morality." And Terry, more than most, believed that all people created in the image of God, are capable of redemption. No one is outside the persuasive power of God's love.

Although his mission left him wide open to criticism, he persevered. He had made a personal pledge to the families and he felt compelled to honor it—at whatever cost in public ridicule and contempt. To mediate in this instance did not mean agreeing with the Libyan regime (although some commentators were happy to give events that connotation). It did not mean seeing eye to eye with Gaddaffi or his policies. It simply meant pursuing his humanitarian goals to the end. And when all formal links with the country were closed, the efforts of one man kept hope alive.

But was he too honest and open for his own good? That question above all hung over his last fated mission to Lebanon. Already it was beginning to be asked in Libya. As one foreign correspondent put it at the time, "He frequently mistakes hospitality and good manners for trust. When the Arabs do decide to trust you, they really do establish a firm relationship. But at first you can't really be sure that what is passing for trust is the genuine article. He is too open sometimes and doesn't see when the Arabs are playing their classic trick—apparently talking to you in confidence but merely telling you what you want to hear. He doesn't speak Arabic and doesn't have a great insight into Arab thinking. Certainly he reads a lot to prepare for a trip, but his weakness is his failing to understand the real nature of some of the characters he is dealing with."

So what some saw as trust others saw as gullibility. Where some saw openness others saw naivety. For the time being at least, however, those questions drifted into the background as success approached.

In February 1985 Terry returned to London, to a

hero's welcome, flanked by the men he had brought back home. His evident integrity had carried the day. For the men themselves the simplest words were the most powerful. "He has done a splendid job," said one, "he has been a source of strength and support to us in the time we have been seeing him. I cannot find words to say other than thank you." Perhaps no more could be said.

Matters did not end there. On his return Terry continued to keep in touch with the men and their families. The Libyan prisoners detained in Frankland Jail, County Durham, were also on Terry's visiting route. He had made promises to look after their well-being, too, and to help their families visit them when circumstances were not easy. The release of the Britons was not conditional on the pastoral care he showed towards them. He had merely promised to look after their interests (guilty of crimes as they were) in a gesture of human fellowship. It had its beginning and end in the fatherhood of God and the brotherhood of man.

"The key thing," said his cousin John Waite, the BBC journalist, shortly after Terry had disappeared, "is that when he starts something he has to see it through. It's a piece of advice his father gave him and Terry often repeats it. The problem is that he has started so many jobs it's difficult to see when he's going to call it quits. You see, in a sense, events in Iran overtook him.

"What people don't realize is that he gets hundreds and hundreds of requests for help. From all kinds of people. Of them only a tiny few might be held hostage and they are the ones who hit the headlines. But every week he and his secretary go through

sackfuls of letters, which he answers personally.
Now, in some cases just a reply will reassure them;
in others he might telephone to offer help or comfort.
And then again if he happens to be on a visit somewhere he will go out of his way to call personally. So
you see, it is increasingly difficult for him to keep up
with all the demands that are put on his time and
energies. If you use the word 'diplomat' he'll laugh
it away. You'll never get him to agree that that is what
he is doing. I think what you would get him to agree
to is that he is demonstrating Christianity in practice—concern for your fellow man, whether he happens to be an Anglican or not."

One thing overlooked in all this, of course, is that
strength that is derived from a deeper source than
mere secular diplomacy. It is the Christian faith that
propels and sustains him. And prayer maintains that
link with the source of all strength. The Book of Common Prayer, much of which Terry knows by heart
from long use, is his constant companion. Its offices
and the Psalms he has memorized over the years, and
in his most recent time of trial these have played a
vital part in keeping him whole.

Interviewed once in a Russian Orthodox church
in London he said that prayer should be "as natural
an activity as breathing," something that connects
you to another dimension of existence but which is
rooted firmly in this world.

That outlook, coupled with his "diplomatic" suc-
cesses, established his unique credentials in a rarefied, uncertain and dangerous world. His grace after
apparent failure and long years of suffering have
merely confirmed them.

Terry's involvement in the Lebanese chapter began in the same year that the Libyan episode ended. It first became public knowledge in September 1985, when it was disclosed that the American Presbyterian Church had sought his help to secure the release of one of its ministers, the Rev. Benjamin Weir. Once again it was church business, but not strictly speaking Anglican church business. With Dr. Runcie's permission, Terry Waite took on the task.

Lebanon was to prove his severest challenge. For one thing, he was unfamiliar with the ways of the country and with the makeup of its capital, Beirut. Here was a once beautiful city that had been systematically taken apart by almost a decade of civil war. And the factions that continued this fighting were far from being easily recognizable. There were factions within factions, family feuds, vendettas, religious and tribal rivalries, petty jealousies, and territorial squabbles that only the experienced could begin to understand.

Wisdom should perhaps have been the better part of valor. With hindsight, most definitely. But in 1985, after such success? And, having been asked, could Terry Waite have refused? Two schools of thought emerge at this point.

The first, that Terry plunged headlong into yet another adventure caring little for his safety, following his own personal star and believing himself invulnerable, when in reality his only protection was ignorance. The other, that he was once again making a commitment to people suffering the pains of separation, and that his only option as a Christian was to offer help when help had been requested.

Either way, he had agreed to lend a hand. There

was some good reason why his intervention might have counted for something. His standing from the Iran mission five years earlier had given him some influence among the Iranian radicals who controlled the activities of the Islamic fundamentalists in Beirut. Moreover, his easy and courteous manner when face-to-face with Colonel Gaddaffi in his Bedouin tent established him as a Christian mediator who was respectful of the Muslim tradition.

Critics, however, say he lacked an important quality: a realistic approach to the ways of the fallen world. They say his naivety blinded him to the depths of human wickedness, so that he simply could not understand how bad people could be. Friends are unwilling to accept that judgment.

"He knows how bad the world is," says Louise Pirouet, his colleague from Uganda. "Living in Uganda at the time you couldn't be unaware of it. And I certainly remember him talking to me about the difficulty he sometimes had in believing in goodness. If you've trodden on the edges of evil, as one did in Uganda, that feeling is not surprising. But he always said that you've got to take the risk of acting openly and honestly with people. However hard it is, you have to try. In the end, he said, you've got to be prepared to give simple goodness a chance."

They are noble sentiments, echoing as they do a feeling that he was taking a risk for God's sake, and that God alone would keep and protect him.

It is true that this alone was not the motivation—individuals are rarely one-dimensional. In so complex a personality as Terry Waite's that was doubly true. So what else compelled him to get involved?

Certainly he is accustomed to taking risks. It is

equally true that he *enjoys* risks, that he thrives on them. Louise Pirouet saw that quality in action first-hand: "He is built to enjoy excitement. I suppose you could say there was a certain *Boy's Own* quality to it. I mean, he would enjoy driving across Kampala when it wasn't one hundred percent safe, and slapping the soldiers on the back at the checkpoints. I'm sure he's matured since then. But in any case the *Boy's Own* element, when it's demonstrated in a responsible adult, can be used to very great advantage. He's courageous—which isn't to say he's unafraid. He's been asked to help the hostages and he has a choice. Does he help them or does he sit back and do nothing?"

In the end, of course, he decided to help in the only way he knew how. Not from behind a desk, as some sort of armchair strategist, but as a man of action prepared to brave the risks himself. He thrived on those risks, as a mountaineer thrives on danger. That was his makeup. As Jonathan Mantle catalogued in his biography of Robert Runcie, Terry would take to declaring, half challengingly, half teasingly, "It's a man's life in the Church of England!" Okay, it was a bit theatrical. But so what?

In America at the time, however, there was another man assigned to the "hostage issue," a fellow Christian, a patriot, a man who courted excitement and danger every bit as much as Terry, but a man who operated on different principles. His name was Oliver North, a Vietnam veteran and member of the Security staff of the U.S. Administration. Their meeting was to prove a turning point in Terry's mission and seemingly led to catastrophe in Terry's life.

But for a time it did not look that way.

8

Dangerous Liaisons

*T*erry was to be brought into the mainstream of hostage mediation after a second direct appeal had been made (via the church in the United States) on behalf of four American hostages held in Beirut: Terry Anderson, a journalist; Father Lawrence Jenco, a Roman Catholic priest; Thomas Sutherland and David Jacobsen, both academics. On the face of it there was no reason for an English church envoy to be involved at all.

Then again, as Charles Glass, former ABC correspondent who himself escaped from captivity as a hostage, wondered ruefully, "What does the guy do? Does he turn down an appeal on behalf of Lawrence Jenco because he's not an Anglican? Or does he accept it and then turn down other appeals because the people don't happen to be Christian? I think he really has responded to humanitarian appeals and I don't doubt his sincerity at all."

Once again, Terry Waite had become a victim of his own success and fame. He had fashioned a role entirely of his own, and the world looked on with apparent approval. He had a simplicity about him that seemed to cut through the usual complexities of international dealing. His presence humanized the abstractions of world diplomacy. It was as if countries and individuals had chosen him as their champion, a solitary Christian soldier in whom their hopes and aspirations were now invested. Here was a brand of heroism that belonged to a less complicated age.

What was particularly risky about this new endeavor was the combination of two such champions: one appointed by the people, the other self-appointed and beyond accountability. Both were brave and headstrong, but where one had the approval of the people who watched him nightly on their television screens, the other was content to work in secret, hatching personal schemes of his own.

At the outset, of course, none of this was known. The arms-for-hostages deal that Colonel North was operating behind the scenes was to remain secret for another year or so. In his book detailing the background to this extraordinary episode, the journalist, Gavin Hewitt, paints a picture of intrigue and double-dealing that appears to have been Terry Waite's undoing.

It has to be said first, though, that it was quite natural that some sort of contact with the American administration would have to be made at some point. Such contact would not, of itself, prejudice Terry Waite's independence. In the complex role of mediator he had to be ready to meet and deal with all sorts of people—from street toughs and high-principled militia men in Beirut to high-level political figures who had access to the levers of power. Mere talking would not interfere with his humanitarian mission. The man had to be informed, after all. But getting in too deep and appearing to play the game by a government's rules (any government's rules) was something altogether different and incompatible with the church envoy's unique ecclesiastical status.

At the beginning there was no conflict of interest. Representatives of the American Episcopal Church (a sister church to the Church of England) met Terry and put him in touch with contacts who they thought would be useful. Chief among these was Oliver North, a devout Christian himself with a background totally different from that of Terry Waite.

For one thing, he had seen active service as a Marine and was as a serving soldier familiar with the ugly realities of war. Politically, Colonel North was virulently opposed to communism as a godless, subversive, and thoroughly anti-American creed. Whereas Terry, in public at least, might have taken a tolerant, middle-of-the-road Anglican position on communism (preferring, if pressed, to temper his feelings with utterances of the "on the one hand, on the other hand" variety). In other words, Colonel North, although fueled by the same desire to see the American hostages back home safely, was also fired by a political commitment that was publicly absent from Terry Waite's thinking. It was a key difference in outlook, which was later to play a crucial role.

The involvement of the Archbishop's man in the current round of activity to free the hostages brought him, whether he liked it or not, into a political arena of such complexity that it called for specialist knowledge. With Middle East powers vying for influence, and prepared to use anyone or anything as a bargain-

ing chip, the person stepping into this political mine-
field had better tread warily. High-minded as they
were, humanitarian appeals alone were a poor trade-
off for hard bargains.

The Americans, for instance, had been kidnapped
in retaliation for the imprisoning of seventeen Shia
terrorists who had bombed the American and French
embassies in Kuwait in December 1983. Guerrilla re-
prisals on the streets of Beirut, involving the spiriting
away of innocent foreigners, were seen as a way of
putting pressure on the Americans to put pressure on
the Emir of Kuwait to release the prisoners. This was
the sticky point. The terrorists were rightly in jail
(they are currently at large or dead following the Iraqi
invasion of Kuwait and the upheavals of the Gulf
War) and to free them was out of the question.

Terry's immediate suggestion was to make it clear
to the captors that he would "look into" the matter
and do what he could to look after the interests of the
imprisoned Shia terrorists on a purely humanitarian
level. The suggestion went down badly with both
sides: with the kidnappers who wanted the release
of their colleagues in arms or nothing, and with the
Kuwaitis who refused to give Terry Waite a visa. And
there matters stayed for some time. Stalemate.

It was clear to both the kidnappers and to the
American administration that symbolic gestures of
goodwill were cutting little ice in the increasingly
protracted hostage saga. Oliver North decided that
the only way forward was to consider a deal. He told
Terry Waite nothing of it.

It was not to be a deal with the kidnappers directly, but with their sponsors in Iran. The Iranian
experiment in Islamic Fundamentalist revolutionary

politics was an experiment they hoped would be copied by other Muslim countries. As a result they were prepared to sponsor groups that would promote it elsewhere. The Hezbollah were their agents in Beirut, and Hezbollah's strings were pulled from Teheran. Doing a deal with Iran might break the logjam in Lebanon. And the only deal the Iranians would consider was a consignment of missiles to help them in their war with Iraq.

Terry Waite has consistently said that trading arms for lives is wrong, that to do so would run counter to his role as independent humanitarian and church representative. It is illogical, too. What good is served by sending one man back alive in exchange for the technology that could send hundreds more to their graves? It was a policy totally at odds with his Christian faith and personal convictions.

And yet, behind his back, without his knowledge, just such a policy was being hatched.

A month after the first consignment of arms had been dispatched to Iran (in a covert operation that was kept from the public and politicians alike), one of the hostages was released. The Rev. Benjamin Weir was a free man.

No one knew what had really prompted his release, but the appearance of Terry Waite by the side of the cleric suggested to the world that "the Anglican Church's Dr. Kissinger" had pulled it off again. True, he had had meetings and discussions (via proper church channels) with some of the key players in the affair, and may have concluded that he had indeed been instrumental in bringing about the release of Weir. How significant those meetings had been no one can be sure. Either way, Terry Waite was content to let matters reflect positively on the Anglican Church's involvement.

What he could not know was that the role he was now playing was ideally suited to the colonel's intention. While Oliver North conducted secret deals to free the hostages (and the deals had to be in secret since they contravened the stated policy of the American government at the time), Terry Waite could be brought in at a moment's notice to take the credit. His presence would effectively disguise the true nature of the deal, take the heat off North, and allow Lambeth Palace to get the glory. It was, in the colonel's phrase, a "neat" arrangement.

When Terry Waite set off for his first visit to Lebanon on November 13, 1985, he was brought into the thick of the hostage drama. Still unaware of his precise role in the subplot of Oliver North's apparent making, he bravely put his personal safety to the test as he prepared to set foot on one of the most dangerous and volatile spots on earth. The factions would have had only the dimmest recollection (if at all) of his success in Iran much earlier, and, anyway, the situation was much different now.

He flew out with the customary retinue of reporters and cameras, but when he arrived he immediately asked them to leave him alone. He needed room to maneuver in his attempts to meet the kidnappers face-to-face. For a man who had no personal knowledge of the situation on the ground, this was courage of a high order. But he went, typically, with the interests of the hostages and their families at heart. It was his personal attempt to share directly in the pain of separation. Having made a promise to help, he shared with them their ups and their downs.

"We have a real sign of hope," he said on arrival. "I believe there is a real possibility of a breakthrough. I'm optimistic but there is a long way to go." Then he was driven off at speed in the back of a BMW by his Lebanese bodyguards.

Later he told another group of reporters in the Commodore Hotel (now defunct but then the base for the Beirut press corps) that he was on the verge of meeting the kidnappers. He could not disclose their identity, he said, for fear of jeopardizing the safety of the hostages: "A wrong move and people could lose their lives." He included in those his own.

His courage in this whole affair cannot be ignored. He was fully aware from the start that he could be considered a prize hostage. He left instructions at Lambeth Palace that if he were to be taken captive, no ransom was to be paid. He came unarmed, alone, and with his personal safety vested solely in his Maker. And for a time he was successful.

He alone was able to meet the kidnappers face-to-face. And very frightening it was: "Normally I'm taken in a car to a deserted building, usually at night. I walk into a building alone. I'm collected by someone and blindfolded, then I'm taken to another location and I have to conduct discussions while someone has a gun in my back." What he did not say at the time was that the captors were so suspicious that he was stripped and examined for weapons, bugs, and secret devices, which, if found, would have left him "a dead man."

However much he had been manipulated by North and his colleagues, he had succeeded in doing what no one else had: meeting the kidnappers. How effective had been his simple protestations of human concern for those suffering from injustice and his appeal to the one living God, we shall probably never know.

Back in the daylight of the everyday world there was no doubt that Terry was enjoying the excitement. He had pulled off a remarkable coup and Colonel North was full of genuine admiration. Unfortunately, the admiration was mixed with other less lofty reactions.

If the colonel could pump the envoy for information, he could consider other actions of his own, actions which he would probably not be inclined to share with him.

Moreover, Terry was now moving into very deep water. Oliver North was at the heart of the American administration, at the heart of the American counterterrorist machine. He dealt with generals and politicians, with secret service officials from the CIA, and with shadowy intermediaries throughout the world. If Terry was now dealing with him, he was in grave danger of jeopardizing his independent status as a simple man of God, an apolitical church representative.

Perhaps he should have understood it all much earlier. The tragedy was that when he did understand, it was too late.

Building on the success of the last trip, a second mission to Beirut followed. What Terry Waite did not know was that a second arms shipment had also been arranged. If a hostage was to be released (as North confidently predicted), Terry would be in place to get the credit and take attention away from the true reason for the release.

During this time Terry Waite was exposing himself to real danger. On one occasion he found himself trapped in his hotel lobby as gunmen fought it out on the streets. He and a group of journalists were caught in the crossfire as rocket launchers were positioned by the hotel entrance. He kept his nerve while bullets flew in all directions but was horrified to see a stray round hit an elderly man at the wheel of his car. He and his wife just happened to be passing and became the latest victims in the seemingly endless civil war. As the wife ran into the hotel lobby screaming, Terry was left to reflect on the senselessness of it all. What, in God's name, he wondered, could be done to bring about peace and understanding.

That, in essence, was the aim of his mission. It had been the aim of all his missions. However much he would eventually be compromised by the Americans, here was a goal of which he never once lost sight.

Back home he basked in the celebrity. But the limelight he enjoyed was not to everyone's liking. There were many of his friends and colleagues who felt that perhaps he was taking the fame too far, playing the public relations game too seriously, and simply falling for the publicity. It culminated in his appearance on a talk show in which he appeared as the talk show host.

It was, to be sure, a disastrous idea in the first place and not of his own devising. He was asked, so he took part. But should he not have displayed a little more reserve, his friends wondered? Laurence Reading spoke for many when he said, "We thought at the time, 'Why are you getting involved in that kind of thing? That's not for you, Terry. The television isn't about honesty. It isn't where you should be.' "

The series met with critical disdain. It was not repeated but acted as a warning that fame could easily go to his head.

It was not that the hostage affair had clouded his judgment, more that his role in it was genuinely invigorating and he wanted to savor every moment of it. It was indeed "a man's life in the Church of England."

It persuaded him that the Anglican Church could have a prominent role to play in world affairs, that it could operate above the parochial level of inward-looking squabbles; in short, that the world would sit up and take notice of what it had to say.

But what of his own role in the affair? Should he not have been rather more astute in realizing that, at best, his impact could only be marginal? The moment of truth was approaching. As Gavin Hewitt makes clear in his book, the moment when Terry Waite might have had serious doubts about his own role first occurred at the time of the release of Father Lawrence Jenco.

Although Terry Waite did not know that it had been secured by a further sale of missiles to Iran (profits to be secretly diverted into combating the properly elected communist regime in Nicaragua), what he did know was that he had had nothing to do with it. And yet here he was, flying to Damascus at Oliver North's instruction, to be photographed at Father Jenco's side. Once again the envoy was publicly taking the credit for things that had been happening, without his knowledge or connivance, out of sight.

Father Jenco was released on July 26, 1986. In subsequent days Terry Waite was constantly photographed with him—at news conferences, at Lambeth Palace, anywhere, in fact, where the association could be made between the priest's release and Terry's efforts.

Later that year a third hostage was released, David Jacobsen. The same arrangements were made. Terry was immediately by his side and photographed at every opportunity. Once again it seemed that the envoy's "magic touch" had paid off and he was not heard to deny it.

There were journalists and government officials who knew better at the time. They had long suspected that all was not as it seemed, and were semi-privately casting doubt on the whole elaborate charade. Between the release of Jenco and Jacobsen those suspicions became public.

For one thing, Terry Waite made a secret trip to Lebanon using American transport helicopters to ferry him in and out. He explained this by stating, quite correctly, that all civilian flights into Beirut had been suspended and (this was not, strictly speaking, correct) that the only way in was by American helicopter.

But what most tarnished the envoy's image was his appearance in Cyprus alongside Oliver North, who observers knew was a highly placed government official—and a "character" in the bargain. Details were beginning to emerge of the scheme to supply arms to Iran in exchange for cash which would go into subverting the Nicaraguan government—another "neat" idea of the colonel's.

The open connection between Waite and North set alarm bells ringing, and raised questions the church envoy knew he would soon have to answer.

Did Terry Waite know of the secret arms deals? No. He could not have consented to act as mediator in an operation that ran counter to his Christian principles. If he did not know, how did he now feel about apparently being used as a decoy, a smoke screen to cover the real nature of the negotiation, which had nothing to do with Christian humility and everything to do with hard bargains and power politics?

At least one man was prepared to support the by now exposed Anglican envoy, and that was Jacobsen himself. "Terry was a man of hope in our darkest hour," he said movingly. "As we sat on the floor in our underwear last Christmas; he gave us hope that we would be free men. We love this guy."

Nothing that the Americans or the Iranians had done in secret could erase the power of those words. What was in doubt was not Terry's force of inspiration, his capacity to inspire hope and confidence. No, what people now wondered, quite reasonably, was whether the Christian mediator had had his efforts (however unwittingly) tainted by hard-boiled political chicanery.

He should perhaps have perceived the whole thing much earlier, but now, at last, he did. He distanced himself from the Americans, denied all knowledge of the arms deal, and was horrified at the very notion. He felt let down. But he prepared to return to Lebanon all the same. It was an action as courageous as it was hopeless.

He was formally warned by the Foreign Office not to return. His employer, Dr. Runcie, advised him against it, but still he went. Why did he do it?

Partly it was to prove the truth of his denial in any shady arms dealing. To return alone would visibly reaffirm his independence as a religious representative.

It was also to honor the promises he had made to the hostage families. Samuel Van Culin was one of the last to spend time with him before he set off: "He felt he had to go. He knew he was taking a chance but he had taken chances before. He said he had to fulfill the commitment he had made to them and their families. When you build up a deep and abiding sense of being integrally involved with the pain, the suffering, and the hope of individual people, you look at danger with less self-caution."

Other close friends echo that human concern: "What he couldn't stand was this intolerable silence," says Gordon Kitney. "When hostages are taken, there are seemingly endless weeks of silence when the family is put through immense torture. And I think that's what spurred him on. He can't stand to see people suffer. And if he can alleviate the pain he will try."

Was there also another reason behind his decision to return? Had not the arms shipments dealt a powerful blow to honesty—Terry's stock-in-trade—and could he perhaps have felt bound, almost by way of atonement, to stake his own personal safety as a deposit on goodness in a bad world?

His journey back to Lebanon was different from all the others. He was weighed down with doubt and fear. The television lights had lost their sparkle. This truly was a real risk. It was a sacrificial journey of such magnitude that it expunged all past folly and misjudgment. It was a personal road to Calvary, the lonely pathway toward an unknown but terrible future.

He appeared in Beirut on January 12, 1987. A few days later he vanished. What he and the world had feared finally came to pass, and for the next four-and-a-half years Terry Waite, who had tirelessly sought freedom for others, was a captive in chains.

9

No Regrets,
No Sentimentality,
No Self-pity

*T*he last pictures we have of Terry Waite before he disappeared for fifty-eight months show a tense and isolated man in the back of a well-used Mercedes. In the front sit his two temporary bodyguards, ordinary-looking in their patterned pullovers. Their nervous scowls and automatic weapons do not inspire confidence.

Tension was certainly in the air when he arrived. Everyone sensed it. Circumstances had changed but only the central players knew to what degree. Journalists and photographers waited expectantly, not knowing what sort of story they would soon be reporting. Terry's future captors, however, knew roughly what the headlines would be in a few days' time. They had plans of their own which Terry himself half-suspected.

Long after the event, speaking in interviews to the BBC, he described those fateful moments before his captivity. He had gone, as had been his routine before, to the apartment of a recognized middleman, a gynecologist and physician to Sheik Fadlallah, the spiritual leader of the Hezbollah. It was at this address that he had met his contacts in the past. The doctor answered a telephone call, turned to the church envoy saying he had a house visit to attend to, made his excuses, and left.

Terry was alone at the most vulnerable point in his life.

He heard the elevator ascending.

His contact emerged and escorted him downstairs to the rain and darkness outside, where he was bundled into a car and driven off to an anonymous apartment in south Lebanon. When he arrived he was subjected to a rigorous search. He was stripped and his clothes examined. Not only that, his teeth were probed for signs of electronic devices, his scars were examined for evidence of secret implants. Had he been carrying anything that might have indicated that he was being trailed by the Americans, he would have been a dead man.

There was a faint touch of irony here. Earlier when he had arrived as unwitting cover for the arms deal, his connection with Oliver North would have been a measure of protection. Now that the whole episode had been made public and the arms had dried up for good, any evidence of some sort of contact with the American state machine they now considered doubly treacherous would have been a certain death sentence.

He was told to wait—not that he had much opportunity to do otherwise—and in that time he felt there was still a chance that he would meet the kidnappers. He waited and waited and during that time he managed to snatch a few hours of sleep. Then he was summarily awakened and blindfolded.

This was the one constant in his Middle East experience—the blindfold. To be kept literally and metaphorically in the dark would be the continuous thread running through this whole affair.

Terry was packed roughly into the back of a van, driven across the city and deposited outside a garage. He was forced through a trapdoor in the floor into an underground prison, of which he said at the time there were many in the Middle East. A huge iron door clanged behind him as he opened his eyes to a tiled cell. "I sat down," he said, "and I knew that was it."

He was a captive.

It was a tiny basement cell in which he could barely stand. He paced nervously around the room like a caged animal, all the time forced to stoop to prevent his head touching the ceiling. They came for him once again, transporting him to yet another location—an apartment in the city. Here they chained him to a radiator. Bound hand and foot he lay totally helpless in the fetal position, unable to move a muscle. They slammed the door, and for the next four years he saw no one except his guards.

In the first few days of his time there he made a resolution to himself. It was a personal promise that was ultimately to keep mind and spirit together: "No regrets, no sentimentality, no self-pity."

For the next four years, as he lay in his cell chained to that radiator, he had ample opportunity to ponder his resolution.

Much earlier, during his time of freedom, he had taken part in a radio broadcast on the World Service of the BBC. In the course of it he was asked to imagine himself alone in a monastery for a period of time. What books would he take along, he was asked, what favorite piece of music would he take with . . . how might he cope with the experience of solitude?

His answer was revealing. First, he said, it would be a welcome relief from all the excitement of his busy life—no telephones, no appointments, that sort of thing. Then he went on to address the more serious issue. It would be a challenge, he admitted. To be alone with oneself, he said, would be a risky undertaking. One would be left alone with some uncomfortable facets of personality and it would not be at all pleasant to have to confront them.

The interior journey would be a sort of spiritual pilgrimage to the heart of one's being, and save for the presence of God one would be dependent entirely on oneself.

He knew well in advance of his captivity that sooner or later he would be facing aspects of himself from which there could be no escape. He would confront his fears, his uncertainties, his guilt, his anger; in short, all those emotions that go into making up the negative, shadowy side of human personality. He had read enough of the psychology of Jung to realize that a person was a mixture of positive and negative elements, which one had to try to keep in some kind of balance. The shadowy side could not be dismissed; it had to be confronted and accommodated.

To do so, however, was a risky undertaking, and in normal times not embarked upon lightly. His incarceration was not a normal period. It was an intense period of isolation during which the discovery of and the confrontation with his shadowy side could not be shared with another living soul. He would be left alone to deal with whatever pain would be encountered along the way.

If he did discover some painful truths about himself (the sort of truths most of us are happy to leave hidden) then he could share them only with God. The flaws had to be acknowledged, forgiveness had to be sought, and the whole of the experience offered up to his Maker. In such a naked and uncompromising state only the truth could support him. In a situation of total powerlessness he could hide nothing from himself because he could hide nothing from God.

He was indeed powerless, with few possessions to call his own—pajamas in winter, a pair of shorts in the summer; no paper, no pencil. For much of the time, though, he had a Bible. And this he read with an intensity he had not known possible. Here was a man who had studied the Bible as part of his professional training, who had read it every day of his life, and who now found himself reading it as if for the first time. He realized that up until this point he had read it superficially. He saw its message in a new light and recognized it as an utterly penetrating portrayal of every single facet of the human condition.

It was as if an unrelenting searchlight had been turned on his whole existence—past, present, and future—a harsh and irresistible light from which there could be no escape.

The only way to survive was to face the truth about himself. "In solitary confinement if you don't live by the truth you wither and die," he said with an honesty that was plain to see. No, he had not known of the arms shipments. No, he would not have approved of them, and if he had gotten wind of them any earlier he would have pulled out of any involvement with Colonel North at once.

He disagreed totally with the policies he had followed, he said, but defended his initial contact with him on the grounds that he had to be prepared to deal with lots of people in the complex business of mediation.

But, yes, he had felt used and manipulated. He had "had the rug pulled from underneath him," but still he had been forced to return to Beirut. He owed it to the families and to the hostages to return. It was confirmation of what his colleague, Sam Van Culin, had said much earlier, before that lonely and perilous return.

He had been asked to help. He could not simply "give in" with a job half-complete. He had made pledges to the families, and to throw in the towel now would have let them down. And, most of all, with honesty compromised by a third party, he felt duty-bound to reassert his own integrity in this whole business. By returning he might—just might—salvage something positive from this wretched, long drawn-out affair.

He looked back on the lost years with no trace of regret. He had followed his conscience and his Christian duty, and done all he could with faithfulness and integrity. He blamed no one. He alone bore the responsibility for the past. He had been prepared to go back to Beirut even though he had known it might cost him his life. But, no, he said, "I'm no great hero."

In a gesture of profound magnanimity he took the mistakes of others onto himself and absorbed the whole episode into his personal experience, saying simply, "in this world there are all sorts of snares." In that plain and eloquent sentence he suddenly became Bunyan's Pilgrim, progressing through life in all its pain toward a goal where all would be redeemed.

The price he had paid for his heroism—if one might dare contradict the envoy's own words—had been heavy indeed. Physical and psychological pain had been almost daily features of his incarceration. Beatings on the soles of his feet with cable ("not to be recommended," he said stoically), sensory deprivation, and complete lack of exercise were only the milder torments.

On one occasion he was transferred to another cell. To do this without fear of discovery they had to hide him. The only object large enough to contain him happened to be a refrigerator. They removed the contents, scraped out the ice, bound him head to foot in tape like a mummy, and stowed him away. As he recalled this frightening experience of in effect being entombed in an airless grave, he remarked with typical (almost unbelievable) good humor, "And I can tell you the light does go out!"

On another occasion he was moved from his cell to an adjoining room. He was thrown into a bathtub and chained to the taps while outside shells began to fall all around. This was a particularly terrifying experience because, unable to move, he could only lie there and wait for the worst. When the building opposite took what he imagined to be a direct hit he figured the worst could not be far away, and again with that characteristic Waite irony, thought, "This is the hottest bath I've ever had."

If he had contemplated death as a possibility, one day in his dark cell it became a pressing reality. He was subjected to a mock execution with no knowledge of course that the threat was not to be carried out. A guard came in and prepared him for his ordeal. "You have five hours to live," he said.

Terry was left alone with his thoughts: "I'm sorry to go like this. I'm sorry for my family," he said. He was allowed to write a letter but realized he needed to write several; to his wife, his children, his friends. So he wrote one to all of them combined, before being given a last request.

Oddly, he said, what he had heard from films and read in books was happening to him. His throat was becoming unbearably dry, so he asked for a cup of tea. The request was granted. He was told to stand up and face the wall. Then a pistol was put to his head. He said his prayers and prepared himself for death. The guard pulled the gun away, turned on his heels, and left the room.

He had, during this time, a number of strategies for survival. One was to go on imaginary journeys in his head. Another was to memorize strings of numbers, or to write an autobiography, and a novel ("several novels") in his mind. But his greatest form of escape was through prayer and dreams. The dreams in particular were a great source of comfort to him. He remembered no nightmares.

Now, more than ever, his subconscious was coming to his aid and the capacity for reflection and meditation that had been as much a part of his personality as the restlessness and the energy came to the fore to offer solace at a testing time.

There were also, he confided, incredulously,

lighter moments—not very many, it was true, but enough to raise a smile on the gentle face of the church envoy. One day he had to be transferred to another location, and a disguise was called for. After some deliberation his captors hit on an idea. They would disguise him as a woman! Dressed from head to foot in the black cloak and veil he could be transported incognito. That at least was the theory. Clearly the spectacle of a six-foot-seven-inch bearded "lady" flanked by heavily armed guards was not the best tactic, and even in Beirut it might have drawn attention!

It seems they abandoned this strategy on future occasions in favor of transportation by refrigerator. The recollection of this bizarre event had both interviewer and interviewee reduced to laughter. That he could still summon humor was surely the best testimony to his immense reserves of spirit.

But his motto of "No regrets, no sentimentality, no self-pity" enabled Terry to bear the experience. It was this rigid discipline, backed up by a conscience that was perfectly clear, that surely helped him to emerge from the imprisonment all the stronger.

And it was as a stronger man that he was determined to emerge. He could so easily have fallen into self-pity and bitterness—a corrosive state of mind which, though understandable, would have diminished him. Self-pity, moreover, would have been able to operate only if he felt himself alone. And Terry knew full well that the Lord would not desert him. With his Bible beside him, and probably from memory, he would have repeated those supremely comforting words from the book of Joshua: "Be strong and of a good courage; be not afraid, neither be thou dismayed: for the Lord thy God is with thee whither-soever thou goest."

With the Holy Spirit beside him he could trans-form the experience into something worthwhile. And as he emerged into freedom that was what Terry Waite resolved to do. The Christian faith, he said, does not lessen suffering. What it does do is convert it; to transform hatred and bitterness into love and compassion.

Through that experience he would come out transformed, better able to understand the suffering of his fellow men and women. He had learned a lot, he said. He could sympathize with the victims of ter-rorism, whether in Northern Ireland or in the Middle East. His time in jail had merely strengthened his resolve to work for the good of humanity, and on behalf of those who suffer.

After four years of isolation as a special prisoner who might be used to exact a special price, Terry was put in a cell with the men whose release he had sought: John McCarthy, Tom Sutherland, Terry An-derson. Although there were tense moments as their close confinement put them all under increasing strain, the likelihood is that such human contact al-lowed them all to acclimatize to the normal world they would all eventually be rejoining.

There were signs that it was already pressing in. At Christmas 1990, for example, they were allowed a special favor. They were given a stub of pencil and a cardboard box, from which Terry Anderson fash-ioned a rudimentary *Scrabble* board. The guards stood over him as he carefully wrote out the letters. When he had finished they all settled back to listen to the radio, and heard with immense relief the

Queen delivering her seasonal message. As she spoke of the hostages and expressed her personal concern, Terry was overwhelmed. "I can't tell you how much it meant to us," he said later, "when she asked for us all to be remembered."

True, it was not the happiest Christmas, even with the *Scrabble* game and the radio, but it was for Terry a moment of communion and part of an experience that would ultimately be put to good use.

Thus transformed, when he was freed at last he was able to invest his words with great moral force. Without anger but with firmness and conviction he spoke out simply against terrorism and kidnapping. There were, he said, legitimate ways to right a grievance. Taking captives was not one of them. Terrorism is a short-term gain and a long-term loss. "Those who perpetrate injustice on the innocent," he said, "will lose their moral force and will wither and die. They will be sapped and emptied."

———

So it was, with four and a half years of reflection and solitary prayer behind him, that Terry Waite prepared to fly back home from the Middle East to England. He landed safely and in good spirits, battered by the experience but not beaten. Of bitterness there was no trace. And as he slid back the door of the Hercules transport plane to take his first deep breath of freedom on home soil, the Church had an envoy of whom it could be justly proud, and in that ecstatic moment the Christian faith had one of its finest champions.